LISTEN
TO THE
VINEDRESSER

31 Declarations Of Who
You Are In The Vine

THERESA M CROFT

KMN Publishing

THERESA M. CROFT

Listen To The Vinedresser: 31 Declarations Of Who You Are In The Vine

Copyright © 2016 by Theresa M. Croft

Published by Kingdom Messenger Network, (KMN Publishing)

3148 Bomar Road

Douglasville, Georgia 30135

To contact the author about speaking at your conference or church, please go to ikingsmedia.com/contact.

Formatting by AnnMarie Stone

AnnMarieStone.me

« Table Of Contents »

THERESA M. CROFT

THERESA M. CROFT

« Introduction »

Life can throw so many curveballs that leave your heart on the floor crushed and bleeding. Amidst a betrayal, a sickness, or death to a marriage or loved one, so many are looking for a Word of comfort and hope. They don't need another trite statement but a life-giving Word from a Father who embraces them with the majesty of His love.

For the past four years I have felt the Holy Spirit speak to me through revelation from the only true care-taker of a heart, the Vinedresser, as He is described in John 15. As His Words came, along with powerful declarations of promises from Scripture, pools of refreshment came to my heart giving me renewed hope, healing, and love.

I started to share these words on my Facebook page or in a blog post, and immediately people were touched as the words of life gave hope. Every time I posted a word from the Vinedresser, I had hundreds of comments and thousands of likes and shares. I knew His Words were touching hearts with a personal word from God, just for them.

So what I found were *real* people longing to hear the voice of God without any religion attached to it. Hungry hearts want to hear an intimate and personal expression from their Heavenly Father that speaks to their purpose and challenging circumstances in life. I understand deeply how you need to be reminded that you are known and loved by God. As a result, when someone hears *a word from God that resounds with their own heart and spirit, they gravitate toward it.*

✟

The purpose of this book is to give you a 31-day devotional of Words from the Vinedresser, based on John 15, with Jesus being the Vine, and God the Vinedresser over the garden. You, as the branch, can hear the Holy Spirit speak. Each day there will be an opening Chapter in the Word. I'd love for you to dig into His Treasure Chest, the Word, and mine some gold for your heart and your circumstance. You will see a word from my thoughts on certain issues of life, followed by a declaration, and then a word from the Vinedresser. If enjoy reading form the Vinedresser and don't want to wait for more, you can visit my Facebook page where I share them daily at facebook.com/TheresaMCroft.

So, I encourage you to come into the Vineyard and nestle close on the trellis of His tender love. He cares about you, the branch, and longs for you to stop striving and simply start abiding... In The Vine. So, Listen...*Listen to the Vinedresser*!

« Your Purpose »

Listen To The Vinedresser

THERESA M. CROFT

Chapter 1

« The Yes Of God »

"Whatever God has promised gets stamped with the Yes of Jesus. In Him, this is what we preach and pray, the great Amen, God's Yes and our Yes together, gloriously evident. God affirms us, making us a sure thing in Christ, putting His Yes within us…" 2 Corinthians 1:20-22 MSG

READ 1 Corinthians 1:17-22

To truly understand your purpose, I believe there is a starting point. You have to say 'yes' to God over your life and then listen to what God's yes means.

What does your yes to God mean…

Gratefulness – Humility – Faith – Belief – Action – Dreams –

What does the yes of God mean…

Favor – Breakthrough – Healing – Miracles – Deliverance –

Or you can think of it this way.

Your yes may mean you check yourself into a detox center. Your yes may mean deciding to repent and turn away from a destructive behavior pattern. Or your yes could be you decide to walk in forgiveness to your spouse, a family member, a friend. Or your yes may mean you simply let go of trying to control everything and everyone and let God take over.

Maybe your yes to God means stepping out in faith to start that business, to trust Him for provision, or to follow a dream, a purpose, you thought had died inside. Your yes to God is one of the most powerful actions you can take.

This yes is not a list or a push that you have to do something. It's more in your understanding of your God-given purpose in life and who you really are in Him, in the Vine. Ask Him to reveal Himself more and more to you. Let Him be your hope, healer, and helper. Let Him direct you in the purpose He stamped into your very DNA.

Your saying yes to God means you will start believing His promises over your life and walk them out into faith. Not sure of HIs promises? Dig into the Word and circle some.

You can start here if need be:

I will never leave you nor forsake you: Hebrews 13:5 (NJKV)

✴ Delight yourself also in the Lord,

And He shall give you the desires of your heart: Psalm 37:4 (NKJV)

✴ The steps of a good man are ordered by the Lord,

And He delights in his way. Psalm 37:23 (NKJV)

This could be a radical change for you because it means your negative chatter in your mind is replaced with declaration of who God says you are.

God's yes to His promises are always yes and amen. Sometimes the yes comes like a no, but it may be simply a delay. He cares more about your heart than your comfort. Don't get me wrong. Comfort comes but it appears in a way where you understand how His Presence brings you peace.

What happens as you say yes to God? You fall so much in love with God. You don't want to hurt His Heart. As you radically say yes to Him, you do not desire the things that used to trip you up.

Declaration: "I am saying yes to God. I am chosen and dearly loved by Him. He chooses Me! He has a purpose for my life."

Let's see what HE says…

Listen to the Vinedresser.

╫

"I hear your yes child. I see your heart that says you are sick and tired of being sick and tired. Just as I hold the clouds in their place in the sky so I hold your worn heart. It's not too heavy for Me. You can do this. You can take that step to forget the haunting past or even the painful mishap that happened just days ago."

"Your yes to Me activates grace, breakthrough, and favor. It's not a doing thing but being. Your yes to Me says you really know who you are in Me, in the Vine!"

"So I really do hear your trembling voice say yes. It may feel like a shallow echo in your soul but it is a thundering, cloud-ripping roar in heaven. Your yes makes my angels stand at attention to move and minister on your behalf. Your yes tears asunder the bars of a prison you may be in…whether it be real or a prison of your own making."

"Your yes is sweet as a grape on the Vine to My ears as I drink the wine of your devotion. So say it again child. Say yes to Me. And watch every yes turn into a breakthrough of my bountiful favor, a bundle of provision, and a peaceful entrance into deeper intimacy with Me. Your yes aligns My purpose for you. It's all meant for you, your destiny by design in the Vine."

Love the Vinedresser

1-4-2017

Thank you! I say YES
to you almighty GOD,
My LORD & Savior by
The Power of The Holy
Spirit! Amen!

Chapter 2

« Called To Reign In Life »

"Then my father taught me, saying: 'Never forget my words. If you do everything that I teach you. You will reign in life.'" Proverbs 4:4 TPT

READ Proverbs 4

I was in deep thought recently about the interesting aspect of one's purpose in life and the process with it. We all have our worries, our doubts, our fears and our own heart pains. Yet, we are called and designed to reign in life!

Whether it's for our children, our career, our finances, each brings issues to the surface.

And we all have our share of speed bumps and smashes in the face with life's cruel realities. A door slams or words are carelessly said. Hopes get dashed in the face of trials that seem to take us out.

I wrote a couple of thoughts down as I pondered this. Let's see if they connect with you:

True heart pain: Feeling like you are on the table in open heart surgery with no anesthesia. This is where you must lean into Him and find a place of true peace and healing.... In the Vine!

Ouch! My daughter knows the shock of pain as she has had to walk alongside friends who are going through some intense heart pain. I see her speak life in compassion and mercy to these sisters. I see her contend with the Word of God in His Presence

You probably could add a paragraph here yourself of some crashes in your life. Good news. God does not define our purpose by the messes.

I am extremely thankful for those who stand with me and my family, as we go through our share of bumps and bruises. I wrote down the following after I thought how God always seem to bring the right friends around to speak life and hope in God's purpose.

So, be thankful for those who see the nuts and bolts of your life and still love you. The ones who take the pieces, dust off the rust, the dirt, and call out the gold. The ones who speak life to you amidst the process of growing up as a much loved Son or a Daughter of the King. Be grateful for the connections who celebrate who you are becoming rather than who you are not. It's in this context of Kingdom family that many will rise to reign in life. With whom is God calling for you to connect with and speak The Father's Heart?

You are designed to reign in life. May I be a voice for you to say that?

Declaration: I can reign in life! This IS THE DAY I walk as HIS Child in the BREAKTHROUGH of accepting His love! I will reign in life!

Listen To The Vinedresser:

"Dear child. I train you so you can reign in life. This is not a striving but an abiding place where you learn to lean into Me and be wrapped around by My Presence. I am your Vinedresser of passionate love. I will give you the joyful strength and empower you to walk in victory over all your conflicts, your worries, your fears.

"Let your resolutions be that you will deliberately strap yourself to the Vine in this garden. Learn the purpose and ways of walking as a child of the King. I guard you. I give you days, weeks, and months of unfailing love. I give

you years and years of reigning. Walk forward in this relentless mercy and empowering truth."

"I Am your quiet and powerful place to hide as you cling to the Vine. I am always more than enough and always available to hear your heart cries and unanswered questions. Fear does not reside in this dwelling place."

✠

"As you learn to lean in-to Me to reign in your life, in Christ, you find the meaning to the process and grow in your identity. The winds may blow, the structure of your faith may shake, and the cold waves slap your face, but you will still stand resolute in a quiet confidence. You know who has the ultimate victory at the end of your glory story of unending grace."

"You are mine, beloved. You are a lover of My Presence. You have learned this secret of not striving but abiding. Dwell, rest, soak; be who I have called you: A son. A daughter who reigns with full inheritance of My Glory in Him, in the Vine."

Love, The Vinedresser

"THEN MY FATHER TAUGHT ME, SAYING: 'NEVER FORGET MY WORDS. IF YOU DO EVERYTHING THAT I TEACH YOU. YOU WILL REIGN IN LIFE.'" PROVERBS 4:4 TPT"

Chapter 3

« Your Best Years Are Still Ahead Of You »

"It's never too late to see God's Hand working in your life to fulfill your purpose..."

READ Psalm 138

God is calling you out. It time to discover your life purpose. To look at your life, the way God sees you.

Let's talk heart to heart. Hopefully these words will empower you. No matter your age your best years are ahead of you!

I really want you to get this: God is so in control of who you are and where you are going. It's the sum of the little things. You can live in doubt and defeat thinking God has forgotten your dreams or you can press on in intimacy with Him and find your true identity. You are a much loved Son or Daughter of the King!

I was struck recently how not having your identity in Jesus can really side track you in your purpose. I was watching a documentary a while back concerning one of my favorite singers from my teens on through my 30's. Her music was so often the back drop to what I was going through in my life. I so appreciated her gift in song writing.

But as I watched this documentary of her life, I was sad that even though she was raised in a Christian home and surrounded by believers, no one really spoke into her life helping her understand her identity or her real purpose. It just made me sad because I know she went through many heart aches, from her marriage to her career. Could that have been avoided? (This is only an observation. Her life is not a tragedy but a beautiful one of grace and mercy).

So here you are reading some of my rambling thoughts about you with the Holy Spirit. Let's talk about YOUR LIFE PURPOSE. No matter your age, it's never too late to see God's hand working in your life to fulfill your purpose.

If you want to see true breakthrough, you are going to have to prepare to see things in the spirit which you have never seen. It's a process. It starts with intimacy. It goes to your identity. Then it filters down to your heart and comes out of your mouth for a total belief system overhaul!

Here is the best news. Your Heavenly Father has great intentions for you. Think of an earthly father and a baby. The baby learns to walk and talk. If the baby falls, the father or mother doesn't say things like...

"You don't have the gift for walking."

"Stay put child. You will never walk. Why try?"

"You will always be a failure and never walk."

NO! The baby gets up and proceeds to learn under the watchful eye of mom and dad who continue to celebrate every step of the child.

That's the kind of attention your heavenly Father will give to you.

I believe now is the time to really pray and ask God to define your specific purpose. (If you already have done this, awesome!)

God has great plans for you, my friend. His Hand of grace on your life says a great deal about His love for you and the quality of life He has put before you. You are made for a specific purpose with unique gifts with which to operate. God put dreams, visions, and wisdom into your hand. Will you talk with Him and allow the frequencies and designs of the Holy Spirit to lead you?

So, get a pen and paper and write what He is saying to you in this special word from The Vinedresser.

Declaration: I am His Kingdom messenger. My life has purpose. I believe God will perfect me amidst the process to the fulfillment of My purpose in life.

Listen To The Vinedresser:

"Dear beloved, did you know I was forming you for greatness even while you were in your mother's womb? I put in your very DNA the longings and motivation for purpose, passion, and perseverance as my chosen messenger. You are beautifully and wonderfully made!"

"Come often into My Heart here in My Vineyard to know that I will not leave you floundering in doubt amidst the process of knowing who you really are in Me, in the Vine. I call you to flourish. Follow me further into the garden, dear one, so I can show you the deep well of my wisdom with all the colors of My radiant love, the power of My tender mercy, and never failing grace for you in the roads you walk."

"The missteps you may take will never define your destiny or leave you in a pit so deep that My love is not deeper still. Reach up. I will take your hand, clean the residue of the enemies lies off of you and set you back in the direction of the Son so you can feel the warmth of My love to heal."

"You are never stuck. Despise not small beginnings. Stay in the soil of My Presence as you hang from the trellis of My care. From this love-filled Presence, I will give you the deep wisdom to talk to the flock I put before you, whether in your home, marketplace, or ministry. Your life will be the fountain flowing with the Father's heart for others to be lead into the Vineyard for their breakthrough. I give you beautiful life-giving words to show others how to walk under open heavens to bring my Kingdom to earth."

"This is my purpose for you beloved. I am here to complete, perfect, and accomplish all that concerns you. The motivation of your heart, the passion and deep longings will find their place overflowing from Me, in the Vine. Lay your

performance and striving on the outside. Simply come inside the Vineyard and abide in the Vine."

Love The Vinedresser

Chapter 4

« You Are Meant To Fly To Destiny »

"Here is the place of peace, intimacy, and total reliance on Me, which I reserve for my godly lovers…" The Vinedresser

READ Song of Songs 2

You may know your purpose but don't understand the delay. I believe often it's a place of preparation. It may be dark and lonely. But don't let go. Stay tucked in His Presence.

This thought of delay gave me a thought of a new name for the Secret Place: The Cocoon of intimacy.

Looking at the definition of a cocoon and its characteristics, solidified some of the thoughts the Holy Spirit was dropping into my heart. For one, He has this special place reserved for you to be protected while going forward in your divine purpose and destiny. It's a place of resting in His Presence.

So while you are waiting, you are tucked into the cocoon of Jesus. He is your covering. Because Christ is in you, you have this seal all over your life. Just as a cocoon provides a wrapping, so God protects your heart amidst the waiting.

Now I know not all of you are in this place. Some of you are fully engaged in your vision. You are out flying high in the purpose and plans of your DNA as you experience your breakthroughs.

But some of you may be thinking: "What is going on here?? How can I be in the sweet spot when I feel stuck in a place that at times feels cold and dark?"

Please don't fret. Let Him wrap His arms around you. You can be found in this sweet spot confident that God is building intimacy with you. In that intimacy you find your true identity, in Him. Let Him cover you and speak intimate tender words to YOUR heart.

He loves you and thinks you are awesome. It's like, you 'hung the moon' type adoration and love from your Heavenly Father. Soon enough you will be flying like you dreamed for your purpose with increased breakthroughs, provision, restoration, and hope.

It's who you are…in the Vine!

Declaration: "I am confident that God is forming in me His perfect designs and purpose for my life. I can trust to wait in the secret place of the cocoon of intimacy of His love."

Now, get a cup of coffee or tea and let's listen to what the Vinedresser says….

Listen to the Vinedresser:

"I'm calling you deeper into intimacy with me beloved, further down the rows of My Vineyard. Here I set you up in a cocoon, protected and loved by My massive arms of grace. I am your hiding place where you can feel My Presence in your times of stress, doubt, and need."

"This is the secret place I've called you to right now, in my garden of destiny. My superabundant grace and revelation cascades over you and in you, in this protective covering. In this cocoon shield, I reveal more of the wisdom from My heavenly realm to equip you. Here is the place of peace, intimacy, and total reliance on Me, which I reserve for my godly lovers. You can see how your destiny is laid out before you and how you can learn how to operate out of a rest mode, with no performance strings attached."

"It's dark in here. I know, child. You may feel totally isolated. But I am watching over you. You are hidden in My strength, wrapped in the majesty of My deep love for you. I only reserve this sanctuary for the lovers of My Presence,

those who truly delight in Me. I have set you high up on this Vine, attached to the trellis of My love, where you are safe and secure before My Face. No dream-killer crows can peck at you to steal or crush your tender heart, nor destroy the DNA of your designed dream."

⸷

"Get ready for My explosive and mighty resurrection power, shooting through your very being, releasing you from restrictive covering. You are being formed to be My advertisement of abundant goodness, grace, and mercy. Your life will be released like a best-selling novel, as you fly under the power of My Anointed One, in the glorious beauty of the many colors of My radiant love. So sit still. No striving. Simply abide now…in the Vine."

Love The Vinedresser

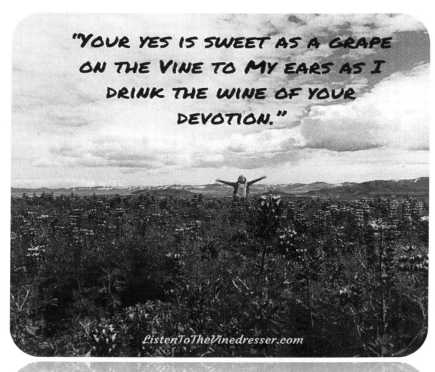

"YOUR YES IS SWEET AS A GRAPE ON THE VINE TO MY EARS AS I DRINK THE WINE OF YOUR DEVOTION."

ListenToTheVinedresser.com

Chapter 5

« Chosen: He Loves You Forward »

"You are always and dearly loved by God!" Colossians 3:12 TPT

READ 1 Peter 2:6-25

Chosen.

As a young athletic tomboy kid, I was always chosen first or second when we divided up to play football at recess. Yes, my friends were mostly guys and my value was in how I could throw and catch a football. (Talk about performance-based-acceptance learned at an early age!)

I guess there was something about having four brothers and being the only girl that put me in a sports circle early in life. I later found the game of golf and excelled to a level that my dear oldest brother had to face. Mike was not embarrassed, but proud, when I played on the same High School golf team!

I was chosen to play on the varsity squad and I'd beat him as a freshman golfer, he as a senior. Bless his heart. He really was precious to me. Mike encouraged me in my pursuit to lose weight, listen to me ramble about my favorite golf players, and take me on his 'short' LONG runs in the winter times.

Ok. Back to you.

You are chosen by God… And you are dearly loved. You are Christ's friend. Think on that. He loved you so much that He laid down His life for you.

When God orchestrates the game of your life, you are always picked and on His team, "the God squad." He doesn't place a value for His team by your performance or your achievements, and certainly not by how much is in your bank account. He looks at you, smiles, and with open arms says, "You are Mine, child. Come on over to the winning side!"

It's simply this. God longs for you to embrace the majesty of His adoring affection. You, loved by God, are on an unbeatable team, friend. He upgrades your DNA to always be a star shining forth HIS love in you for others to see.

He puts a label on you: You are a much loved son of the King. You are a much loved daughter of the King. He has purpose for your life. You are His shining star.

Now is the time for you to take a step in faith and fulfill what the Vinedresser has put in your heart for your purpose and destiny. It's really not about you, but about the people God has called you to impact. God has woven His love and greatness in you. You are not out of it.

He's asking you to jump in the river (Holy Spirit) and trust Him amidst the process of your purpose in life. It's easier to flow with the river than try to control it. Try as you may to direct this river, fear traps you, the banks get mushy, and the river becomes a stagnant swamp.

But, if you're trusting God and flowing with the Holy Spirit, you are going to see amazing things. Yes, you will have to find the right strategies that create the winning results. Yes, you have this stamped in your DNA and you can do it! And yes, you are chosen to be on the winning team

Declaration: I am chosen by God and dearly loved. He has upgrade and purpose for my life. I am on the winning team.

Listen to the Vinedresser:

"I will always love you. You are dear to Me. Did you know I chose you before the creation of time and had you on My mind? You are divinely chosen to be called My holy lover with an unstained innocence, joined to Me in the Vine. You are selected and ordained to be a part of My goodness, partake of My inheritance as you are joined to the Vine."

✝

"I gave you your destiny. It's stamped into the very core of who you are in Me. Even while you were formed in your mother's womb, I was shaping you for your divine purpose. I watch you like an open book; all the pages of your life were spread out before me. I dropped a warrior-spirit in you, which lines up with the core of My DNA, with its fire and passion for excellence."

"You can trust Me to perfect it through the times of momentary messes and strange circumstances. I am not moved by these moments, beloved. Your times are in My Hands, in the Vine. For you are wonderfully and marvelously made. You take my breath away."

"My plans are for you to prosper, be healthy, enthused with the purpose of My heart for you. As you walk in this destiny, you are My vessel to bring heaven to earth with all its glory and power. You are accepted My dear child. No rejection here. You are on My winning team. So walk in this calling with confidence. No striving, simply abiding, in the Vine."

Love the Vinedresser

THERESA M. CROFT

Chapter 6

« He Is Worth The Climb »

"When Jesus saw his ministry drawing huge crowds, he climbed a hillside. Those who were apprenticed to him, the committed, climbed with him. Arriving at a quiet place, he sat down and taught his climbing companions." Mathew 5:1-2 MSG

READ Mathew 5

My visits 'in the vineyard' often revolves with time writing on my blue tooth keyboard, connected to my I-pad, and the Word of God open. Thoughts from my journal with Holy Spirit often produce words from my Father.

God is really awesome about helping me express His thoughts on issues and situations that you may think about amidst your day-in and day-out display of life. Many *"Listen To The Vinedresser"* words come from this intimate place as I lay my heart bare before the Lord. Other times they are birthed out of praying for you!

Lately, I have enjoyed different translations of the Bible that the Holy Spirit lights up like fireworks in my heart. I always am impacted by the Passion Translation, but recently the Message Bible has been rocking my world. I was reading Matthew 5 and came to this conclusion for myself:

"Jesus is my one true guide and teacher amidst the process called life. I desire to be relentlessly committed to the pursuit of His Presence (Holy Spirit) so I can clearly hear His voice, even if it's a climb at times."

How about you? Are you one of the 'committed ones'? What climbing have you faced? May I encourage you to NOT put away your heart-hiking-boots and keep reaching for His Voice and His promises.

You may really be in the midst of a climb right now. It might be soul wounds from past devastating events in your life. You can find healing to be made whole.

My husband reminded me of this fact:

"There is an anointing which causes the Kingdom of heaven to invade earth. Walking in your true identity facilitates the doorway to healing. On the other side of healing is wholeness. You become whole so you can help bring healing to someone else!" -Firebrand Dave.

Look at every problem as a chance to see a promise of God and a possibility. If the struggle is with people, especially in your immediate circle, think on this: If God shows you negatives about people, He is charging you with responsibility to be the voice, to execute the kindness into that person's life. You have the spirit of breakthrough. You are the gift of God in their life.

Declaration: I am one of the committed ones. God has deposited His Spirit into me to encourage others, even those who get on my nerves. I have the gift to take the high road and speak life as I walk in kindness.

Listen to the Vinedresser:

"Will you travel with Me, dear child, up steep hills and through dry desserts to hear My voice? I long to teach deep wisdom secrets and sweet revelation to those who are relentless to travel further into what seems the darkest place in My vineyard."

"Here all is still. Here you feel the very branches of My Presence wrap around you. You are so wrapped in My Anointed Vines that the slightest movement reveals my gentle healing touch."

"This is a place for my committed ones. Here you feel the very tender beats of My heart as I speak intimate words of never ending hope, peace, and love. Here you realize what you thought was lost, what you thought was most dear to your heart, is replaced with an embrace in this secret place."

⧾

"I have great deposits of faith to pour out on you as you unwaveringly seek who you are in the rows of My garden. Your steadfast pursuit here will be rewarded with a healed mindset and a renewed passion for what I put in your very DNA. Come, My intimate companions, and find how blessed you are, in the Vine!"

Love the Vinedresser

Chapter 7

« Milestones Of Purpose »

"Fix your heart on the promises of God and you will be secure, feasting on His faithfulness." Psalm 37:3 TPT

READ Isaiah 54

Recently, I've been encouraged to go over chapters in the Bible that are Biblical milestones in my life in regards to my dreams and purpose. As I thought back to the past three decades, these chapters jumped out in my mind. Psalm 34. Psalm 37. Psalm 84. Isaiah 54 and 58. John 15. 2 Corinthians 9.

I was reading Isaiah 54 again and a rush of memories came back. I was single and needing a deep soul healing. One memory came to me while I was at the beach on a singles retreat. I had gone out into the ocean only to be tripped up by a huge wave and slammed into the sand, coming up a tad embarrassed with a mouthful of sand. It hurt too.

That night God had me camping out in Isaiah 54. He spoke intimately to me with assurance He loved me and would bring the healing, the husband, and the children at the right time. I remember this verse so well:

"O you afflicted one, tossed with tempest, and not comforted, behold, I will lay your stones with colorful gems, and lay your foundations with sapphires..." Isaiah 54:11 (NKJV)

Can you relate? Do you feel storm tossed by the craziness of your circumstances you are facing or the soul pain from mistakes made in times past? Do you have dreams and hopes which you wonder if ever will manifest?

God can make sense amidst the madness and the wait. Cling to Him. Find healing in His Word and in His voice (Holy Spirit).

╬

So, along with the struggle, and at times raw pain, know God is working. This is no time to lose hope. He has you and will complete what concerns you. Listen! Do you hear that? It's the lover of your soul, the Vinedresser, speaking to you. First, let's make a declaration!

Declaration: I know that God is working in me for His purpose. I do not need to lose hope. I am His and He will perfect me.

Listen to the Vinedresser:

"I sing over you dear child. Now, I am asking you to sing and to break out into a joyful loud song. I am moving in you for deep healing and real hope. As you remained in my Vineyard, the soil of My Presence is making you ready for more, far more than your wildest dreams or imaginations."

"Because you have patiently waited even amidst desolate times, this upgrade is upon you. Get ready. Clear lots of ground in your section of My Vineyard for what I have set for you. I'm calling you out to take over whole nations and resettle abandoned cities with My Presence."

"Your time of covert operation in My gifts is bringing in your heart's desire. No need to be afraid or be embarrassed. I will be there for you so you will never come up short. This is your divine design time. Yes, child, this is for you. Soon you'll forget about the humiliations and shame of your past. Your misery has paved the way for your destiny. You have clung to the Vine as your Redeemer God. With enormous compassion I'm bringing you back with a faithful love that will never end."

"I am rebuilding you with precious jewels as I make your foundation firm in me. You will live in great peace and be secure far from terror. If any should

attack don't believe the lie that I sent it. Nothing will come of it. Darkness is as light to me, child. No weapon can hurt you. I will silence every accusing voice raised up against you. Stay here in the Vine. I am your vindication. I will see to it that everything works out for the best. It's who I AM, in the Vine."

Love the Vinedresser

THERESA M. CROFT

Chapter 8

« Your Secret Name »

"He who has an ear, let him hear what the Spirit says to the churches. To him who overcomes I will give some of the hidden manna to eat. And I will give him a white stone, and on the stone a new name written which no one knows except him who receives it." Revelation 2:17 NKJV

READ Genesis 1

Recently I was going through some struggles of the heart. The negative chatter in my thoughts were trying to dominate. I know the best way to strengthen myself is with praise and thanksgiving in my heart as I contend for the promises. I do not like the smell of fear anywhere near my dreams.

What are you facing? May I be a reminder that God is working in you always for your best interest? He has your cares and your life carved out in a secret place where you are completely known, with a secret name, that delights His heart.

A secret name?

Check out this verse:

"He who has an ear, let him hear what the Spirit says to the churches. To him who overcomes I will give some of the hidden manna to eat. And I will give him a white stone, and on the stone a new name written which no one knows except him who receives it."

Revelation 2:17 NKJV

He knows you, friend. He has your times in His Hand. You can find thanksgiving in the Vine, in the sweet spot.

The Holy Spirit spoke so clearly a few days ago that I needed to remind you of this simple truth.

Prophetic word for you right now: There is a better day ahead. Let the process shape you and not discourage you. You have a good reason for hope to be kept alive because God has bigger and better plans for your life. He has breakthroughs for you! He is working ALL THINGS together for your good!!! He loves you!

Make it your declaration!

Declaration: I know better days are ahead. I trust God as I journey through the process. I will not be discouraged because I can have hope God is working to match my purpose with the fulfillment coming in days ahead.

Listen To the Vinedresser:

"Beloved, listen to the wind words of My Spirit. I am for you. As you chase after Me, you will find your visions for your future coming true. When you learn to live from heaven to earth, you will experience my intentionality for your life that drips with favor and, like a fountain, overflows with satisfactions."

"You can expect better days ahead. Your trying circumstances are part of the upgrade process of learning to bring My promises and provisions to every problem. I have breakthroughs ahead for you because I put My breaker anointing in you. You have good reasons for always having expecting-hope because My enduring love follows you with goodness and mercy. As you grow more intimate in your love for Me, I show you more of the majesty of My love for you. It is resplendent and full of glory."

"In this intimate place, I will give you provision to conquer the giants that pester you, those issues that sidetrack you with pain. You can overcome beloved.

Just as David ran after Goliath with five smooth stones, I give you a white smooth stone inscribed with your new secret name which no one knows except my Spirit. With this name I define your true identity. You then, start to live from a place of rest, from a place of victory. You proclaim who you are in Me in every circumstance with joy, confidence, and thanksgiving."

╬

"So, dear child. All you have to do is believe and receive. No performance needed for Me. You simply walk out the characteristics of who you are, in your new name, in the Vine. I love you, dear beloved. I have you. I won't drop you. I am here for you....in the Vine."

Love the Vinedresser

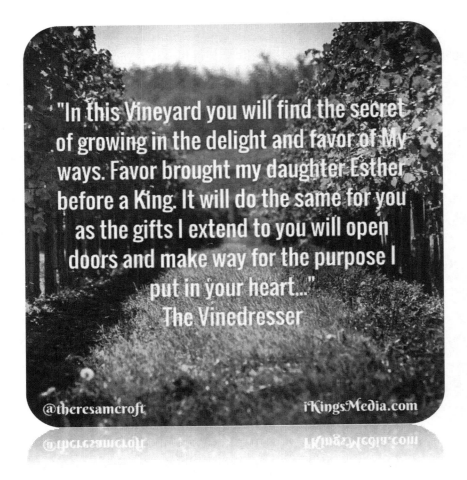

"In this Vineyard you will find the secret of growing in the delight and favor of My ways. Favor brought my daughter Esther before a King. It will do the same for you as the gifts I extend to you will open doors and make way for the purpose I put in your heart..."
The Vinedresser

@theresamcroft   iKingsMedia.com

THERESA M. CROFT

Chapter 9

« You Are A Revivalist »

"Your idea of fun is drive by blessings or walk by healing..." The Vinedresser

READ Acts 3

What are you going through? Do you feel your dreams and purpose are forgotten by God?

May I encourage you? His plans and purpose for your life are huge.

There is a better day ahead.

Let the process shape you and not discourage you. You have a good reason for hope to be kept alive because God has bigger and better plans for your life. He has breakthroughs for you! He is working ALL THINGS together for your good!!! He loves you! You are His much loved son, His much loved daughter!

I believe that as you dream with God you need to see something in your purpose that seems so impossible that you would need God to pull it off.

I'm serious.

It's who you are... in the Vine, in Him. He has deposited His Holy Spirit in you to walk with signs and wonders as a normal event. Think of it this way friend. The same POWER that raised Jesus from the dead is alive in you!

You are His Revivalist!

I truly believe God is pulling people from the wreckage of fear and devastation of tragedy and raising them up as beacons of light. From upheavals in marriages, to crashes of finances, nothing is too difficult for God. Messes do not move Him off His throne and make Him powerless.

There is a better day ahead.

So, I am challenging you to rise up from the ashes and start to speak of who you are in Him. There is power in the name of Jesus and power when you speak His name with HIS PROMISES for the purpose of your life.

Intercession removes depression.

I believe you are pregnant with a dream that is so majestic. Yes, it hurts when you are pregnant and overdue for birth! (My son was a week late and I thought I was going to die from the pain!)

Abide in His rocking chair in faith by that open window. The misery you may feel now will be the path of your destiny to touch thousands with your 'baby'. Don't grow weary. I understand you are tired. Strengthen yourself in your faith.

Will you say this with me: "I am a Revivalist!"

God is calling you out. He is putting His Finger on your heart saying you can't hide this, child. I have put it in your very DNA to move mountains with the faith I have given you. Everywhere you walk you will change the atmosphere with the open heaven that is above you. Heaven is not something you are waiting for, heaven is NOW, as you abide in that intimate place with HIM!

The Holy Spirit told me to share this word again…from the Vinedresser about you!

Declaration: My life has purpose. I am a revivalist!

Listen to the Vinedresser:

"You are My revivalist child. I give you the deep revelation to fruitful activation to make you My messenger to impact thousands. I have touched your life with an extraordinary solution to someone else's pain point. Yes, the desire for the manifestation of your true destiny is from Me."

╬

"You have learned to patiently wait in My peace room, the Vineyard, and find what you really long for: More of Me. Gentleness now resides in you. You have learned that nothing can satisfy the last aching abyss in your heart like the tender love of Me you experience in My Vineyard. You crave righteousness and are surrounded with abundant fruit. You demonstrate tender mercy with grace and have learned to unselfishly spill that same grace out to others."

"Your idea of fun is drive-by blessings or walk-by healings. You choose peace over strife. Instead of offense you choose forgiveness. Because you have walked with me in the realm of My Kingdom by hanging out in the secret place, My Vineyard, I have endued you with power to live victoriously in every area of your life."

"You become the breakthrough. You are the shift for favor. You carry the glory story. You are connection because you are connected to the Vine. You are revival because revival has blown through your heart disrupting the chaotic plan and pain of the evil one. You are My revivalist because of my abiding Presence."

"You are the much needed salt to a world which has lost its appetite and hope for a loving meal at My table. You are light to a world who thinks darkness is normal and struggles with enmity and conflict. Being a revivalist is not about striving child, but simply abiding. My Presence in you is able to defeat any opposition you may face in your mind or in your reality."

You are My Hands to bring salvation, deliverance, and healing to the world. So say it child, "I am a revivalist!" It's really who you are… 'in the Vine'.

Love the Vinedresser

« From Despair To Hope »

THERESA M. CROFT

Chapter 10

« He Will Turn The Titanic Around »

"It might take a little time now to get back on the ground, takes a little time now TO TURN THE TITANIC BACK AROUND..." Song By Amy Grant

READ Hebrews 12:1-3

Recently, in the middle of the night, I awoke suddenly to the sound of waves, the words of the Holy Spirit and a memory.

Dave was serving and working for a dear cousin at an island in Florida, so I had the blessing of receiving sweet revelation, downloads of words from Holy Spirit on long walks on the beach all week long. I was definitely feeling like a much loved Daughter of the King as this trip was rather sudden and unexpected.

I not only heard His voice often while walking, but also an unusual amount while sleeping. If anyone knows me, they know I have the GIFT to sleep and sleep hard rarely waking up. So, I love it when God does wake me up to speak a strong word....AND helps REMIND ME what He said.

This one night I woke up rather abruptly. It came with a distinct word and a memory from years ago that I had totally forgotten about.

First the memory: I was deeply troubled, terribly stressed, and really questioning God about some issues going on in my life quite a few years ago. I felt cold, desperate, and lonely. And then this song came on as I sat in my car wallowing in my fear. I felt the Lord directly say this to me…from an Amy Grant Song… "It might take a little time now to get back on your ground, takes a little time now TO TURN THE TITANIC BACK AROUND…"

I remember hearing that lyric and this peace enveloped me and invaded the trouble beats of my heart. I felt Him push back my fears instantly. I just knew He WAS GOING TO turn the Titanic of the troubling issues around and I was to simply believe!

So, here I am years later, sound asleep with the sounds of the ocean out the window when I awoke not only to this memory, but also a realization God answered this cry of my heart. Then the Holy Spirit spoke a word that shook me to the core as I realized He had more than turned the boat around. He brought MORE restoration than I could ever imagined. He said something like this, *"Don't let the pressure of the process keep you from pressing on with My promises."* He told me I needed to share that word with you.

I had trouble going back to sleep, but I eventually did to the sound of the waves and a tender heart. I was so moved by this memory and the way that God cared for me as He kept His promise. He is so much more intentional about loving us through the process for progress than we could ever imagine. We are His much loved Daughter. His much loved Son.

I explain more in this video which you can find at this link: ikingsmedia.com/turning-the-titanic-of-troubles-around. I hope you can watch it. I believe there is a word in it for you. Yes, I awoke the very next morning, grabbed my camera and shot my thoughts…by the sea with the noise of the wind (sorry) and the sound of crashing waves.

I did ask the Holy Spirit if The Vinedresser had a word also. The answer was a resounding yes.

THERESA M. CROFT

God is all about helping you through the process and progress and not expecting you to walk with the chains of perfection and performance.

Get a pen and write this declaration down:

Declaration: I can expect God to turn my troubles around. He will help me through the process to progress as His much loved daughter, much loved son.

⊥⊤

Listen To The Vinedresser:

"Dear child of Mine I see the raging troubles of your heart as you face the high waves of rough seas from your circumstance. More than that, I hear your desperate plea for help. I am here as your mighty stronghold in the day of your raging troubles where you feel you can't even help yourself right now."

"I am here. The pain of the process has a purpose for progress in My Kingdom. Come closer to Me in this quiet place in My garden and let me gently speak My confident hope and breathe Holy Spirit Wind of strength into your lifeless sails. I am a safe warm place from the storms and a shadow from the heat of the process of the pressing issues pounding your heart."

"Know that I rule the stormy sea and its angry waves. As you cry out in faith, I am at work in your heart. Yes, even if you feel you have no faith at the moment, I can still glide across the out-of-control waters drowning your hope, no matter how fierce the gale of winds are blowing."

"It might take a little time, sometimes, but I will turn the titanic of tribulation and trials around. I hold you close, child, as you wait for the turn around. The time will be the process to perfect you in your faith in the Vine, in Christ, and you will see progress and restoration."

"Now fix your eyes on Me. I am the Author and Perfecter of your faith. I will accomplish what concerns you. Your concerns become My concerns. You can trust in Me. Your times, your life, are in My Hands. I will not drop you, dear one. You are My daughter. You are My son. I will not forsake the plans and purposes of My laid-down lovers. Though you may not see it right now, I am turning it around. If you have fallen, here is My Hand to pick you gently

up. No pit is so deep that My Hand can't reach down and pick you back up with tender mercy and compassionate care. I will never let you go."

"Remember child, you come from a place of victory in Me. At times, it may feel like I'm asleep in the boat, but I am not. I have set you apart for a time such as this. So, let Me give you the eviction notice to your fears and doubts. Cease striving and rest in the abiding. You have a secure place in My heart, in the Garden."

Love the Vinedresser

THERESA M. CROFT

Chapter 11

« Crashes On The Heart »

"What the enemy used to destroy you I will use to upgrade you in the Vine..." The Vinedresser

READ Psalm 91

About a year ago I experienced one of the biggest crashes of the heart and arrow to my dreams. When that happens I often go to the Word and my computer (journal) to process. I will unashamedly share here, hoping you might relate or might find hope in the word from the Vinedresser.

This sudden unexpected moment has brought out the tender love of my husband for me. He has so empowered me to fly and not stay grounded.

And it has brought out the gift in having real Kingdom connections, friends who gently speak words of life. Their love and support is such a gift from God...all resplendent with His Glory.

I'll spare you the details but the core is simply this:

One of the most difficult things in relationships, in business, is to be misunderstood.

When someone accuses you of something that is NOT at all in you or in your spirit, it can hit like an arrow ripping through your heart. When it involves a dream, it can make you feel like you drove your car into a brick wall.

Crash!

How do you take the thrust of the knife on your heart and turn it around for good?

I know of only one place. It's in the Presence of my Father with the Holy Spirit doing the surgery to mend the bleeding, ripped open heart. As I push back the orphan spirit that wants to be justified or wants to stay in a state of depression, I rise and run to the Vineyard.

Yes, it's here, in the healing Presence of Holy Spirit…where I simply abide…dwell…rest…embrace…and be upgraded in my identity.

Declaration: I can take the crashes on my heart and give them to Jesus. His comfort is enough as I hide in the secret place.

Then He so gently speaks to you…

Listen To The Vinedresser:

✳ *"My beloved, come to Me and rest under the shadow of my tender love for you. Give it all to me child. Yes, take your mind off the crashing blow. No need to try and figure this out. No guilt or performance on your part is necessary. Now, allow Me to gently remove the sharp cutting arrow from your heart. My Spirit will be the Balm of Gilead that not only takes the sting away, but also makes you whole. Lay the betrayal you feel in emotions down on the altar as a sacrifice and move on. Let your dashed dreams of what this might have been be a sweet savor to Me."*

"What the enemy meant to destroy you I will use to upgrade you in your true identity…in the Vine. You can contend with the enemy with My Great and Precious promises. My promises are designed to release you from fear into joy, from a foot soldier to a warrior."

"Fix your eyes on me, dear child. The place in your life where you feel the crushing blow on your heart, that wants to take you out of the garden, will

become the greatest place of your intimate encounter with Me. This is your time for upgrade as you rise to occupy a higher place in My affection!"

✟

"The place of battle dear child can be the ground for fresh sweet revelation of who you are becoming in the Vine. You learn to go from seeking a visitation from Me to enjoying habitation IN ME while you enjoy even more territory in this Vineyard. I'm singing over you, beloved, as I embrace you with my wrap-around compassionate Presence. Watch as I place more of the majesty of My love on your life! More fruit will come from this painful pruning moment. Now dwell here in my embrace. Rest in My victory. No strive child, just abide. ...In the Vine!"

Love the Vinedresser

"YOU ARE NEVER STUCK. DESPISE NOT SMALL BEGINNINGS. STAY IN THE SOIL OF MY PRESENCE AS YOU HANG FROM THE TRELLIS OF MY CARE."
THE VINEDRESSER

ListenToTheVinedresser.com

THERESA M. CROFT

Chapter 12

« The Pruning Brings The Healing »

"Prune me to ruin me from lustful longings, from passing passions, and prideful pleasures. Break me to make me more like You."

READ John 15

I'll be honest. I have not wanted to touch on this subject of pruning simply because I feel so many have the wrong picture of their heavenly Father. He is not a task master. He does not expect perfection. Even in the midst of our messes, He still calls us radiant.

You can read the Song of Songs to get a clear picture of how He is relentless in pursuing us and calling us beautiful. Song of Songs 1-5. I suggest you read it in the Passion Translation!

For the pruning part, check out John 15: 2 (NKJV)

"Every branch in Me that does not bear fruit He takes away; and every branch that bears fruit **He prunes**, that it may bear more fruit." (My emphasis added with bold text).

What do you do when your struggles seem to never end? What do you do when the very thing (stronghold, issue, sin) you think you broke off remains? Where do you go when even your close friends seem to have lost patience with you? How do you get into the 'sweet spot' amidst the constant rattle of the battle in your mind and your body?

This is the pruning process. It's the trimming away from the old way (tradition), breaking off strongholds, and cutting away the bruise in the fruit. It's the removal of those things that can destroy your destiny. Fear. Pride. Control. Lack (spirit of poverty).

I've learned a lot by reading how important it is to a Vineyard to prune in the off season. If a vine keeps growing without being pruned at the last place of bearing fruit, it will continue to grow out using all its 'energy' to keep growing, but with no fruit. I think to myself: *"How often do I refuse correction and use all this energy in my process of life with no fruit to show for it?"*

As I wrote in my book *'In The Vine'*:

"I have learned not to be depressed about the process of being pruned for fruit, for harvest. Sometimes out of what seems the most devastating situation or worst betrayal, Holy Spirit moves in powerfully to speak to me." This is my heart's cry amidst this process of pruning:

"Lord…I desire to be IN THE VINE…living life by design, not mine."

"Prune me to ruin me from lustful longings, from passing passions, and prideful pleasures. Break me to make me more like You." (In The Vine: Living In The Vine, In The Sweet Spot).

Just some thoughts… Bottom line is, God is interested in our progress. Will you trust Him with the pruning process to bear more of His fruit?

Will you be quick to forgive?

Declaration: I can trust God's loving Hand in pruning me for my own character. He loves me enough to prune me, not ruin me.

Listen to the Vinedresser:

"You can't hide from me, beloved. When you run from me thinking I will rebuke you, I remain constant in My tender love for you. You are my radiant

one. Yes, I call you radiant even when the mud of the world has been caked on your face with worry, shame, disorientation, offense and fear. I don't leave you in that state but invite you into the Vineyard for training."

If you feel the sharp cut from the pruning process, know that this is evidence that you are my delightful child. My Word cleanses the pruning wound with relief from My faithful love through this process. Welcome My gentle Hands as they handle you with care through correction. For just as a father corrects his son, so I will correct you. Take this pruning mark as your validation that you are My much loved son, My much loved daughter.

✝

My pruning is an invitation dear one to share in My holiness. The pain is relieved here in the warm garden with the oil of the Holy Spirit flowing over your tender places that hurt so badly. Look for the transformation child as the refining of your character brings you a harvest of righteousness, peace, and restoration.

You are beautiful and radiant Child. Come now and leave your fear of rejection and pain from arrows from others. I am here to love you forward and over the mountains of troubles. If you ever lose sight of Me, just follow My footsteps in this garden. This is where I lead my lovers to the sanctuary of My flowing river spilling over with healing waters. You are mine in the Vine. You are My radiant one!

Love the Vinedresser

Chapter 13

« Rejection To Correction »

"Truly my soul silently waits for God; From Him comes my salvation. He only is my rock and my salvation; He is my defense; I shall not be greatly moved." Psalm 62:1-2

READ Psalm 62

We have all faced it in one form or another.

Rejection.

You might have been rejected by a mother or father. Or maybe a spouse walked out the back door, or stomped on you.

How do you deal with rejection?

I believe this is an ugly spirit that rises up from a root of fear in an orphan spirit. This is someone who does not know their identity and continues to fall into a pattern of wrong behavior. They may have the truth of being loved by their Father in their mind, but there are crevices in their heart where it is not fully manifested.

Even a mature Christian can trip up by this spirit with certain issues that bring back that feeling of rejection.

Personally, I don't have all the answers. Not even a handful.

But, I do have His Word and the ability to soak asking for revelation in overcoming rejection in the Vine.

As I was praying the other day, He spoke something basic I could do. He told me to be like the tribe of Judah and go forth in battle spiritually in praise and worship of Him. That means, to magnify Him, and not the spirit or feelings associated with rejection.

╬

Praise and worship breaks the bars on any heart and keeps an open heaven atmosphere around you with peace, hope, and more revelation. Think on this: Because Christ lives in you, you are the open heaven wherever you go.

Of course, I really love when the Vinedresser speaks…

Declaration: When I feel stomped on in rejection? I know God is near to comfort me…in the Vine!

Listen To The Vinedresser:

"Your feeling of rejection makes you say and do things that can hurt others and yourself. Come to me my child. Rest in My arms and let me remind you of how I see you. As your heart feels a deafening thud which leaves you shattered and broken, this is when I am most near. I am here to save you from yourself with your stormy emotions, your crushing blows. Listen, beloved. Even if your father and mother abandon you, I never will. I take you into My Vineyard and surround you with healing songs of enduring love, hope, and peace. You have my assurance that I deeply love you and you belong…in the Vine. You are Mine."

"Don't give up, child. Don't lose your patience or anger. Be wrapped, be entwined with Me. You will find courage in Me to be brave and never lose hope. Even the sting of My correction can be sweet. You are meant to bear much fruit, so despise not the knife that cuts away the bruise from the fruit and trims the branches (you). In this painful process, I will never walk away from

you. You belong in the Vine. I will not forsake you. In this storm of life, I softly speak, 'I love you'."

"Release your emotions on Me, child. When you scream out that you feel shattered, helpless and doomed, I rush in with My fiery love to rescue you. Come closer. Here you can lay the troubled beats of your heart and soak in the soothing comfort of My Presence. I am your true tower of strength, your safe place, your true shelter, your hideout, your tree fort high up in the Vine. I am near. Miracles are possible. No strive. Simply abide. In the Vine."

Love the Vinedresser

Chapter 14

« Curve Ball To The Heart »

"Even the sting of My correction can be sweet. You are meant to bear much fruit so despise not the knife the cuts away the bruise from the fruit and trims the branches (you)." The Vinedresser

READ Psalm 61

Life throws you a curveball and you are reeling with emotions. Maybe you found out someone was talking about you behind your back. Maybe it was a disagreement with a spouse or friend. Or maybe your child just told you he hated you.

How do you deal with the emotions?

Sometimes you have to process by worship through difficult situations in your life. I see my 18-year-old daughter do that more as she grows in her intimacy with Jesus. She may come to me with a circumstance that is really doing a number on her heart. I'll simply ask her, "Have you worshipped through on that, Anna?"

Then there is my husband. He processes through early morning hours of prayer. And I mean early. Many, many, times he's up at 3 am and 4 am while I snooze away praying. He also goes one more step in this by talking out what God is showing him. I've learned to be a good listener.

I had a major speed bump recently dealing with feeling total rejection. Just like my daughter and my husband, I had to shift through my emotions. While they sing or pray, I write.

I used to have a journal. After having two boxes full of journals and handwriting I can barely read (yes, my own), I have gone to the keys of a computer. Usually it's my I-pad connected wirelessly to my Logitech keyboard.

╬

So I mused all day through the emotions of a situation where I felt rejected by someone who with whom I used to have contact. She was like a mom and a friend wrapped into one.

As my heart soaked its open wound in the Word, my fingers began moving on the keyboard. The Vinedresser began to speak to me.

Can I share it with a declaration? Maybe it might bless you or you have a friend going through a rejection. Please feel free to share it.

So, I open a row of vines in the vineyard of my heart, some with grapes, some with branches that have recently been pruned, as I share this with you:

Declaration: I can take my pain with offense to My Father. He can heal the hurt and put me back on my feet!

Listen to the Vinedresser:

"Dear precious child of mine, let my love nourish your heart. Bring your raging emotions to me. The pit you feel in your stomach is not from My garden. The rejection you experienced is only a speed bump in the pathway I have set before you. I call you My intimate friend. My overflowing love will never disappoint."

"My tender love handles your fragile heart as a priceless tea cup. Even if the cup is carelessly handled or dropped and scatters into countless pieces, I am here to gently clean each fragmented piece and mold it with mercy and

compassion back together. I am near. Lean into Me. When you come into My garden, the anointing of My Presence will satisfy you and heal your crushed heart."

"I also have other Vines, other connections around you, who speak My Kingdom revelation to aide you in your journey of love. You are never deserted or alone, dear one. I have a grip on your life and My Presence is always here…in the garden. Abide. Soak. Be strengthened in My love."

Love the Vinedresser

« Growth Through The Process »

THERESA M. CROFT

Chapter 15

« No Performance Needed »

"Answer this question: Does the God who lavishly provides you with his own presence, his Holy Spirit, working things in your lives you could never do for yourselves, does he do these things because of your strenuous moral striving or because you trust him to do them in you? Don't these things happen among you just as they happened with Abraham? He believed God, and that act of belief was turned into a life that was right with God." Galatians 3:5 MSG

READ Luke 10:38-42

Mary or Martha? Let's have some coffee!

Are you a Mary or Martha? If you're Martha, I'll take my coffee with a little bit of sugar and creamer.

Mary? Grab a chair let's talk about Jesus. Martha can join us too.

I will have to admit I've been more of a Martha in my Christian walk. I'd get so irritated when my husband would say things like… "You need to come from a place of rest Tee"…or he'd say something, lovingly, about my performance-based acceptance mentality.

You know what I'm talking about? It's like you only feel good about yourself if you are doing something. You do, do, do, instead of be, be, be. You know the result… You end up in a cruddy place instead of a peaceful one. You end up stressed and depressed. You experience and feel lack instead of abundance and joy no matter your circumstances.

I've been there. Done that.

But in the past few years I'm slowly learning that what God accomplished on the cross is a finished work. He doesn't need what I do for Him to determine my self worth.

Religion will try to grab my neck and then I think I must jump through the hoops of that mentality. One example: If I miss my normal quiet time in the morning, I'm going to have a terrible day.

But I'm learning more and more about His Kingdom. Kingdom means you never take off the hat of a lover of Him and His Presence simply flows with you throughout the day…regardless of missing your 'quiet time'.

Kingdom means the Holy Spirit can still flow when I go to the grocery store with my husband.

Kingdom means you declare His promises over your life and walk them out in faith. As you strengthen yourself in the Lord amidst this process you come to find real transformation. No greater example of this is when you have a belief system radically changed.

I saw this one part of a verse Galatians 3:5 in the Message translation:

"He believed God, and that **act of belief** was turned into a life that was right with God."

My heart leaped. A declaration was formed. Ready? Get a pen and write this one down!!

Declaration: Believing the promises of God is more important than striving to work to please Him. I can walk in patience knowing God will fulfill His Word in my life.

Listen to the Vinedresser:

"Dear, dear, precious child. I see you. Your persistence to perform and keep up a religious front is truly wearing you out and confusing you. Listen, my

child. Allow My Spirit to blow this truth deep down into your weary heart. Simply believe the touch of My Presence will empower you to walk in My ways. I will give you the patience amidst the waiting for the promise to be fulfilled."

╬

"The only job you have is to believe and be. Believe that I have poured out the lavish supply of my Spirit into your life giving you the miracles of My tremendous power. Be who I have called you to be. The being does not come in striving but abiding. Out of the overflow of all I give with My sweet blessings and grace-filled power, you will possess the promise in your patience. Now go forward in this promise to your destiny of being a world-changer."

"Come closer, child. Let me hold you now. The crash of trying to please Me and others has taken its toll. Let Me breathe on you now a new measure of grace to be who I've called you to be: A lover of My Presence. It's who I've made you to be. It's who you are, in The Vine."

Love The Vinedresser

Chapter 16

« SEA OF TROUBLE »

"The Son of God is always shining on you. He is coming out from the clouds of your circumstances. He is breaking forth now. You reflect so much of His glory. Everyone around you will have to put sunglasses because you shine, you reflect the resplendence of His Majesty, you mirror heaven." The Vinedresser

READ Mathew 11:28-30

I can remember this amazing heart wound a few years back. It felt like I got whacked by this huge wave (in my professional life) and came up hurt, sore, and eating sand.

When the waves of life crash in, where do you go? You may feel too much pain has smashed in on you right now. Emotions of recent hurt, abuse or betrayal has you on the floor crying.

Or you feel that no sooner do you rise above for air, the next wave slams you down and you end up hurt with sand in your mouth? Devastation from what has happened freezes your faith. One too many tidal waves with massive winds have hit the sails of your hopes and dreams. You may even start to sabotage the goodness of God coming in because you have trouble forgiving yourself?

It's good to cry. I'm glad you can be real. I hear you and have felt the same pain. I'm sorry you have to face this trial of gut wrenching proportions.

But…I see you coming out of this mess with a message. I see gold in you amidst the fire of the process. You are not defined by what is in your past but by what God has deposited in your spirit. He put Christ in you. He is there to pick you up, carry you, and love you forward.

The waves will not always slam you down.

I think God is asking you to float with Him and ride the wave

He sees the breakers of the sea storms that are throwing you down. God is mightier. First, He is asking you to float, to totally trust Him. Next, He wants to show you how to surf. Come to Him and hand over all these troubles and worries.

From sky to sea, He is there to pull you up and out of any struggle.

Walk with Him as He steadies you with His Word of promises.

So that's what I feel God is saying to you right now. Walk with Him. Keep in step as He steadies you with His promises and His everlasting love for you.

The Son of God is always shining on you. He is coming out from the clouds of your circumstances. He is breaking forth now. You reflect so much of His glory. Everyone around you will have to put sunglasses because you shine, you reflect the resplendence of His Majesty, you mirror heaven.

Ride the wave friend or float. No matter, He has you…in the Vine.

Declaration: I have strength in God to endure any overload on me trying to take me out of the vineyard, whether it's from work or family issues!

Listen to the Vinedresser:

"I see you My child. The wear and tear from your daily struggles is wearing you down. Sea storms are up. Yes, I see them wild and roaring with thunderous breakers throwing you head first into the sand. I am stronger than wild sea storms child. Mightier than these sea storm breakers."

"Will you float while I carry you now? That means come to Me with all your cares and demands from others and be robed with My Presence. In that quiet place in the Vineyard I will show you My Face, reveal my tenderness in love, and manifest a true strength to fill you with hope."

✝

"I see you Child, from sky to sea ever ready to pull you out of the ocean of overload and turmoil. The waves are not stronger than Me. I rule surging with strength from My Vineyard ever ready to come to the rescue of one of my lovers. Walk with Me now. Keep in step as I steady you with My Word of promises, my everlasting love for you, in the Vine."

Love the Vinedresser

THERESA M. CROFT

Chapter 17

« Delays In The Well Of His Presence »

"When you're in over your head, I'll be there with you. When you're in rough waters, you will not go down..." Isaiah 43:1 MSG

READ Isiah 58:11-14

Delays.

I don't really like them. I don't like to be delayed at the airport. I certainly do not like a delay on the interstate.

And obviously no one likes to be delayed in their destiny.

But could this be part of God doing some deep work inside your heart?

I believe so.

You are born for something that's on the other side of an opposition or challenge. It's who you are in the incubator of His Presence.

For one, God wants you to learn to rest in Him. In this place, healing comes to your body. You learn to lay your burdens down and find a peace in His Presence knowing you are NOT alone.

What delays are you feeling friend? What deep waters do you feel you are in? Could you believe that you can find HIM in this place?

Let me share a different kind of word from the Vinedresser that you may need today.

The bottom line is He trusts you in this place.

I had spoken this prophetic word to a young man at church Sunday during worship. Days later, God brought that word back to me as I was hanging out in Isaiah Chapter 43.

I was praying and processing some issues in my own life. I believe you can relate to being anxious or fearful. God spoke THE word again to me, and He told me to share it with you. Ready?

Declaration: God has not forgotten me. Even though I face delays I know He is working all things for my good.

Listen to The Vinedresser:

"You do not have to be afraid. I have bought you with a price. I have called you by name. You are mine. Even if the water around you is cold and dark, I am still here. Do you trust Me to drop you deep down into the well of My Presence, My pleasure? I have the rope and I will not drop you."

"Where I take you the water is sweet and refreshing. If you try to climb the rope back up the well, the water will be bitter. So do not press and strain. I am taking you to a deep place in the well of My Heart."

"I trust you with this process. Few are patient enough to be dropped to this level of intimacy. It may seem cold, damp, and lifeless. It is not. You will learn that My Presence is here to warm your heart with My peace, to bring light and hope amidst the waiting."

"I have not forgotten you. Nothing will compare to what I am going to do. I am doing something new and it's beginning to happen. You will find a refreshment that will spill out to others. I trust you with this pure water, this message. As I refresh you, I cause you to refresh others with words of life. Hold on now, child. The sound of the drip in the deep well is your assurance I am here."

Love the Vinedresser

Chapter 18

« Keep Hope Alive »

"Quiet your heart in his presence and pray; keep hope alive as you long for God to come through for you." Psalm 37:7 TPT

READ Psalm 37

My son has this wonderful habit. He asks me often, "Are you alright, Mom?"

No matter what I may going through, I always answer in a positive...

So, he asked me again today. I stopped myself saying I was anxiously waiting (for a phone call or notification on something very important) and again said, "I'm fine, Will."

Shaking my head, knowing I had an early morning of real struggles and doubts, I went back to the Word, looking over the 'milestone' chapters I had been perusing. Instead of checking my email on my phone for the 100th time, I knew what chapter to go to.

Psalm 37

So I dug in...easing the anxiety tension inside with the soothing life giving words of God.

This verse stuck out:

"Quiet your heart in his presence and pray; keep hope alive as you long for God to come through for you." Psalm 37:7 TPT

Keep hope alive. That has to be a 'now' word for today. And the way to keep hope alive is so simply laid out in this verse from the Passion Translation... Get in His Presence and be still, pray and proclaim the goodness of God over your life.

I knew the Vinedresser had something to say about this...and a declaration:

Declaration: My times are in God's Hand. I can trust Him with the dreams of my heart. In my patience I receive His promises.

Listen To The Vinedresser:

"My child, come into My Vineyard with your fear filled anxiety and gut-wrenching worry. Take your eyes off what you are waiting for and rest your heart on the secure promises I have spoken over your life. Keep hope alive. Come to My banquet table and feast on my never ending faithfulness."

"As you learn to taste and see how good I am, you can walk daily making My Presence your utmost delight and exquisite pleasure in which to leisurely bask. I will provide what you need and even what you desire the most. Your hopes and dreams are as alive in My heart as they are in yours. After all, I am the Creator of them."

"See My Hand reaching out to you? Hand over the reins dear one, and give Me the right to direct your life as you trust Me along the way. You will find that simply managing your relationship with Me is so much easier than trying to manage people and the circumstances around you. I have a way of taking problems, stress and fear away from you, pulling it off perfectly."

"Keep hope alive child. Let me be your justice. As sure as the sun comes up each day is as sure as you can be of my righteousness and acts of grace with

favor. Shhh. Be quiet, dear child. No need to explain the whys and the how's... Simply come deeper into My Vineyard away from the arrows of anger, envy and revenge. They won't hit you here in My Presence. Take a seat. Let's talk."

⊹

"Do you remember all My great and precious promises. Reflect here on testimonies of past heroes and present day Kingdom messengers. Do you see what happens? My Love makes your hope come alive. As you make Me your total delight and pleasure, I have this way of providing exactly what you desire."

"Stay in the Vineyard dear one and give Me the right to direct your life. I will appear daily as your Hope. I will manifest righteousness, justice and provision. Keep hope alive. It's here...in the Vine!"

Love the Vinedresser

Chapter 19

« Dreams Coming True »

"Now to Him who is able to do exceedingly abundantly above all that we ask or think, according to the power that works in us..." Ephesians 3:20 NKJV

Read Ephesians 3

I am a dreamer. God plants these huge ideas in my mind and I want to accomplish them.

I have a dream of making my Facebook page an outlet for healing, prophetic words, deliverance, and amazing amount of HOPE to spill out every day. I also dream of helping Kingdom-minded businesses and messengers do the same with online media.

I can remember as a 7 and 8 year old climbing the steps of our home making it my pulpit and preaching to the grass. If there was an empty apple cart, I'd tip it over and be a tent revivalist proclaiming to the rocks and flowers they need to repent and follow Jesus.

I loved microphones. Back then the modern technology was a tape recorder and a mic. I'd sneak my Dad's recorder into my room and talk into the mic as Walter Cronkite, or try to be funny like Carol Burnett.

Give me a mic and I wanted to say something positive. I thrived on it so much that I volunteered to be a 'reader' at my local Catholic Church. They had a microphone!

Now some 4 decades later after a 15 plus year stint in Christian radio and still at a mic on my computer, the destiny continues.

God has stamped in your very DNA a specific purpose with a passion to be secure in the Vine, in the sweet spot of your destiny.

You have a purpose. It might be that burning passion or love for something that no matter how you try to ignore it, the dream still burns like an ember in your heart.

Ask God to stir your heart if you feel you lost your vision.

Some days walk through the valley of discouragement. Other days I may have to face the negative critics who say it can't be done. (By the way, these people are not in the grandstands of my life. I am thankful for my family and a few close friends there who are waving their white towel cheering me on).

But if I am truly honest, the biggest enemy to my dreams is my own mind.

So I had a talk with the Vinedresser. Guess what He told me? He said I could dream with Him because He gave me an imagination to visualize and dream big. So, in line with the purpose of speaking life, which has been stamped into my DNA since birth, I thought I'd share this with you.

I believe God is raising up His Kingdom people to dream big and setting them apart by the breaker-anointing that flows through His Bride. You are part of that remnant! Look for how God moves on your behalf. Give Him glory and watch it bounce off of you to others around you. Keep dreaming, keep trusting! Watch God move on your behalf toward your dreams!

Take a hold of this declaration and dream!

Declaration: "I can dream with God. My imagination is active for the purpose of God in my life."

Listen to the Vinedresser:

"I have called you my dreamer child. I have made you intelligent and discerning in knowing Me personally and to truly grasp the immensity of the glorious way of life I have for you! Do you know the extravagance of My ways to work in you? Do you see the colors of My love wrapped around you?"

✠

"I give you endless energy, boundless strength to make your dreams come alive and be real. I give you confident hope in Me as I have called you to my glorious inheritance. Dream my child! I will often flood your imagination to experience this great hope of glory."

"Your life is My billboard displaying My love, My hope, My delivering power for all to see as I work in and through you. Walk in your dreams every moment as you plant your thoughts and imagination in the soil of My Vineyard for Kingdom greatness. Plant your thoughts here, not in the cesspool of the world, pride, or your past. I am the fulfillment of all your dreams! Let them grow here in the Vine! No strive. Simply abide."

Love The Vinedresser

THERESA M. CROFT

Chapter 20

« Connections In The Vine »

"Once you leave the concept of family, you have lost Kingdom." Bill Johnson

READ Proverbs 27:9-19

I believe any true connection starts in the Vine, from an intimate relationship with Jesus.

So I ponder this thought:

How do you write about something that is on your heart with fresh insight?

I've written before how God is raising up family, friends, and heart connections as a factor to help Kingdom families reign in life as we share the Father's heart. I believe 15 minutes or less releasing the Father's Heart in love to someone can have more impact than years of sermons, seminary, and the like. (Not to discredit any of such venues of learning and sharing the Gospel.)

Recently, I witnessed someone who walks this out (Todd White) and saw the result of such a lifestyle. As Todd says... "I'm not about religion but relationship...with God... People are not an inconvenience but an opportunity."

So as the enemy tries to ramp up resistance to this with envy, strife, betrayal, abuse and other bad fruit that can happen in relationships, I believe God is rallying His Kingdom Messengers on a mission of faithful connections.

"Once you leave the concept of family, you have lost Kingdom." Bill Johnson

Recently, I wrote this '*Listen To The Vinedresser*' after four days working and fellowshipping with two very good friends. I don't have biological sisters but God makes up for that with friends like these. As I thanked God for my family and a few friends I could count on to really speak gut level honestly with me for growth, I realize how 'running with your tribe' is so important.

When you align yourself with people burning for the same Kingdom walk, you are encouraged and strengthened.

These are the kind of friends, who have your back, who will fight for you, who will be faithful and never stop praying for you. No matter how messy things may get in your life, they will still honor you for who you are and not judge you for who you are not. These kind of connections also refresh your heart just by being in their company. I love this verse that explains this so well:

"Sweet friendships refresh the soul and awaken our hearts with joy, for good friends are like the anointing oil that yields the fragrant incense of God's presence." Proverbs 27:9 TPT

Be intentional with staying connected to these ordained relationships. God never intended for you to walk alone.

"It's better to have a partner than go it alone. Share the work, share the wealth. And if one falls down, the other helps, but if there's no one to help, tough!" Eccl. 4:9-10 MSG

"If you want to grow in wisdom, then spend time with the wise. Walk with the wicked and you'll eventually become just like them." Prov. 13:20 TPT

Here is another word in the Vineyard to remind you God knows you long for restoration and for real friends, connections who will love you through any process. He is about relationship.

Declaration: I trust you, Lord, to align me with friends who burn with Kingdom love and will encourage me in my destiny.

Listen to the Vinedresser:

"Dear child, I understand when hope's dream seems to drag on and the delay for real connections and restored relationships seem nowhere to be found. I am here, dear one. Put your arms up and let me pick you up and hold you as your heart aches from a stone thrown, an arrow shot, or a word that bruised."

🕆

"Hand over this pain that has shattered your heart. Forgive and release those who have hurt you."

"Allow the beats of my heart to remind you I am close even when you feel lost in the coldness of isolation or crushed by betrayal in a relationship. Let me pull the arrows out and pour the oil of My spirit in that gaping wound. The process may seem like it is slow but know the timetable is in My Hand."

"I am all about restoration, connection, and validation. As you receive the first connection in an intimate relationship with Me, there lies the fulfillment for your heart's longings. Find it with Me first. Stay clinging. Keep hoping and believing."

"I am about relationship Child, not control or performance. This is not an inconvenience, but the foremost intentionality of my Heart for you."

"Now as I set you down, let's dance. In the rhythm of grace, I put a song back in your heart. Stay in motion to the sweet tune of My overflowing love. You will find your real love in Me. Yes, this can be a slow dance at first as you learn to hear the beat of My heart in tenderness for you. When you are ready, you can twirl and dance like David danced."

"Look dear one! As the healing comes in your own heart, look for those gems in friends I bring across your path. From the overflow of your first love with Me, connections will come. It's how I designed you, being connected to Me, in the Vine."

Love the Vinedresser

THERESA M. CROFT

Chapter 21

« Activation To Dreams »

"LORD, by Your favor You have made my mountain stand strong."
Psalm 30:7

READ Jeremiah 29:10-14

It was quite a few years ago when I felt in shambles on where to go with my burning desire to work and help messengers share their message online. It was something I could not shake. It was in my DNA to speak life and help others with their media movements for the Kingdom.

One hot afternoon I took my tired and weary heart to the kitchen table and sat down to watch Patricia King on my computer. I saw the heading, 'God's Media Army' with an interview with James Goll. As Patricia and James began to speak and share the movement of the Kingdom media mountain, my heart burned and leaped. I sensed the Holy Spirit speaking to me.

Their message and activation of this media ministry vision was like drinking a tall glass of water after weeks in a desert.

At the end Patricia had a prophetic word. She peered into the camera lens and her words pierced my heart. I knew God was speaking to me through this word of knowledge.

I remember her saying to not give up, because God hears the cries of my heart. And even though there had been mountains of opposition, God would make a way, that His favor would be on me. She ended her word with Psalm 30:7

"LORD, by Your favor You have made my mountain stand strong."

I knew the journey was just a new beginning of sorts as I got up from the table and heard the Lord say, *"Yes, your vineyard can be ministry marketing online for the messengers…"* I dug in again and continued my earnest online marketing training, all the while being immersed in the Word with my desire to know more about God's Kingdom.

I remember one day after this video encounter, my husband started to call me his 'fruitful vine'. I never had mentioned the vineyard thought to him and was tremendously encouraged. It was like God gave me a kiss with those words as Dave continued to call me his fruitful vine.

You may need a kiss from God like this example.

May I encourage you to shake off the lies and false agreements running through your mind. Break off thoughts like these…

"Favor is determined by what I do and my performance of being good."

"No one in my family has ever had any good luck (favor)."

Start believing that today is the beginning of God to show His favor! Look up the promises He speaks about you. You are an heir! He gives you an amazing inheritance sealed by the Holy Spirit in Christ!

As you go through the process of life and continue to cling to the Vine, God has this way of upgrading your life with more favor. Look for it. Believe it. Walk in it.

Your dreams still have purpose in God's heart. Your desire for healing, provision or restoration has not been forgotten. Favor in these areas is all about relationship.

Continue your relationship with God, lean on the Holy Spirit, and expect drops of His favor around you. Look with the eyes of your heart, not your mind. When God speaks to your heart you will know it because His Spirit will leap inside of you.

Some of you simply need to let Him hold you. The Holy Spirit will cry with and for you. In this embrace comes healing and refreshment.

The Vinedresser loves you and longs to pour His tender, extravagant, compassionate love and favor on you right this minute.

╬

Declaration: My dreams have purpose in God's heart. He will give me the favor to walk out my dreams and experience His breakthrough.

Listen to the Vinedresser:

"I wrap you, dear one, with my unlimited favor and canopy of tender love. The glory of My splendor is pouring more tenacious strength into your life. My marvelous favor lifts you high as you become a magnet for more of My kindness and approval. You don't have to strive for this favor, dear child. It's found in the intimacy of abiding with me through the process of life."

"Because you steward well the favor I pour out each day, I will entrust you with even more tomorrow. Celebrate My blessings on those around you and watch the rebound effect. The favor I lavish on you becomes tremendous breakthroughs for you in your family, your health, your finances."

"My magnetic favor cascades around you reaching out to everyone with whom you come in contact. You become the joyful carrier of My glory as the anointing I place on your words and actions extends this favor to others. Despise not the small things. Be found faithful."

"Stay clinging to the Me and get ready. I have more extravagant generosity…in the Vine."

Love The Vinedresser

Chapter 22

« Now Faith »

"God has stamped in your very DNA a specific purpose with a passion to be secure in the Vine, in the sweet spot of your destiny…"

READ Hebrews 11:1-6

Recently I had a strange battle with my health. But in my weakness, I spoke out faith. "Now faith is," my heart shouts. I believe. I have soaked in this song for over a week that Bethel sings, a version of the song King of My Glory.

"He never falls off His throne," sings Steffany Gretzinger (with Jeremy Riddle) as she prophetical sings in the middle of the song.

Awesome words containing a faith power bomb for my heart as I watch on a video.

I sense many feel slapped down. You may have an attack going on with your health, your children's health, finances, relationships. I read one prayer request that so touched my heart of a mom coming from work to a home with three sick children and a bursting pipe pouring water into her house. I pray earnestly as my heart goes out to her.

The assignment against you is not greater than the faith in you. Your weapon is the declaration of His Word. What does God say when the enemy crashes your mind with negativity?

This thought made me think of this phrase I said to myself over a year ago:

When fear freezes faith, anxiety slaps you in your face, or panic replaces peace... Take courage. He still walks on water. He still moves stones...

So that's a simple reminder for you. I encourage you to continue to declare what HE says. Your faith will arise as you listen to the Word of Your Father, declare His promises over yourself, your family, and as you walk in belief. And offer up thanksgiving and praise.

This faith will not fail you. You can go through any storm and be able to sleep in the boat just like Jesus. How? Why? Because you are coming from a place of victory as a much loved son, a much loved daughter of a King. Victory lives in you. You can call forth what is in heaven and see it manifested on earth. It is really who you are. In the Vine! Need more encouragement?

Declare this and then *listen to the Vinedresser*:

Declaration: Victory lives in me because I'm in Christ. I have faith to believe His promises. He never falls off His throne. He is so good. He will never let me down.

Now Listen to the Vinedresser:

"I see the weariness on your body dear child. Come out of the cold of your circumstances into the warmth of My embrace in this Vineyard. Look into My eyes that shine radiant love for you. Listen to My heart that skips a beat as you hold fast to Me. Listen to the truth of My intentional goodness when I tell you I never train through pain."

"I am here to pour into you more of My tender kindness, rays of sweet revelation light, and soothing comfort to quiet the ache of your tired heart. I am showing you a shining path that leads you into My burning Presence, where sin, lack and doubt drops off."

"Repeat often My Word of Life I speak to you, to replace the clang of doubt that beats you black and blue. Offer on the altar of your heart thanksgiving."

"I have a flowing fountain of strong faith springing in you. I am the light of Your holiness. Refreshment comes from me in honest confession and humble thanksgiving. I keep pouring out My unfailing love to you as you hang on to Me. I am here to release more blessings as you remain loyal to stick like glue to Me, as you cling to the Vine."

⁜

"Not once have I forsaken a lover of Mine. Keep moving forward and steadily in My Ways. Can you hear Me? I'm singing over you a song of a new day. I have set you free. Many will see the miracles and breakthrough that is coming from your faith in Me, in this quiet place, in the garden. Many will stand in awe and wonder of how I have healed and restored you."

"So again I say, 'keep moving'. I have placed Victory in you. I have deposited a 'now faith is'. Word into you. Your life is ablaze shining My glory. You are like a brilliant billboard set high displaying the majesty of My blazing love for all to see. You carry the testimony as a son, as a daughter of the Father. You give others hope for more of His glory stories as you bring heaven to earth. It's who you are in not striving but simply abiding…In The Vine."

Love, The Vinedresser

« Breakthrough To Destiny In The Vine »

Chapter 23

« Breakthrough Starts In The Heart »

"Why are you down in the dumps, dear soul? Why are you crying the blues? Fix my eyes on God—soon I'll be praising again. He puts a smile on my face. He's my God." Psalm 42:5 MSG

READ Psalm 42

The place of breakthrough starts in the heart.

As I go forward with writing and listening to Holy Spirit, I have come to realize how important the heart issues are.

Recently, I produced a Video series called, ***The Place Of Breakthrough***. Amidst attacks on my health, I went to take a nap one day. So with thoughts to God to help me find His wisdom for breakthrough, I laid my worn out body on the bed.

Instantly Holy Spirit started downloading a framework for breakthrough. I remember thinking... *"This is real good God. Will you help me remember this when I wake up?"*

The next day I had to lay down again to rest and God brought even more clarification to this word.

It was so specific and so simple to follow without feeling like you are striving or having to jump through steps. It could be integrated into any lifestyle and any problem where you need breakthrough.

I have no doubt this download was from the Holy Spirit. I find myself having to go through the steps the Holy Spirit share myself as I wrangle with issues that have been so tender on my heart. I will tell you that I have failed. I have found myself in a pity-party or totally stressed out.

Be moved by His Presence, not by the outward appearance of your circumstances.

That's what Holy Spirit dropped on me amidst all these emotions as I spend some time in His Word.

I hear the cries of many as I peruse media outlets as part of the assignment He has put in my DNA. My heart says contend for this media territory. He tells me to not be silent and to cry out for more of Him.

So once again I go to my keyboard to write my heart.

Is this you?

You're tired. The dissolutions of your circumstances are many. You are not even sure if God hears. May I encourage you? Don't lose hope. Hang on to Him. Contend for your dream. He will not leave you in the valley but raise you up to handle your destiny.

One thing you can do friend: Give thanks, praise, worship. Declare His Promises; walk by faith and not your emotions. This is not to get anything from God but simply to experience His Presence and receive the fellowship of His Spirit. Make sense?

God says, "Contend for the territory in your life to which He has called you. Cry out for more of Him to come in and transform your life. The birthing process can be painful and messy. Stay connected to Him and watch for the breakthrough in your family, finances, dreams, desires, and destiny."

Sometimes your ambition gets nipped. It's not to destroy you but perfect you amidst the process of His assignment for you. What may feel like a valley is the heart training ground to learn the tender love of your Father, and learn the joy of obeying His voice.

The secret is the secret place found entwined in the Vine listening to the Vinedresser.

You are not forgotten. You are not invisible. Find the joy of who you are in the Father's Heart....in the secret place, in the Vine!

╬

I wrote this Vinedresser word below amidst all this. I found so much life and comfort in Psalm 42 which led to this word:

Declaration: I will fix my eyes on Jesus. I will offer up a sacrifice of praise and thanksgiving.

Listen To The Vinedresser:

"You can enter My garden with your out-of-control raging emotions and your wreaking with fear questions. Messes do not move Me. Your intercession in the Spirit does. If you feel you are banging your head on the same wall getting nowhere, why don't you try walking down the rows of My Vineyard with Me? I have no walls here, only My Presence to overtake you and heal your shattered heart."

"I am using the process to promote you not press you down. I am near to the broken-hearted. I save those crushed in spirit. So come dear Child and sit in the quiet with Me. Release the troubled beats of your heart by talking with Me. Intercession in the spirit defeats depression."

"Why are you sinking into despair? Why the tears making your coffee salty? I am your towering mountain of strength. My promises are flowing to the point of cascading and drowning out every problem. In My garden is a safe and powerful place. I am more than enough. Watch as I pour into your heart-wounds more of the deep kindness of My tender love."

"Remember, beloved, My resplendent glory will overshadow you as you enter in to My Vineyard. My majestic love will wash your tears as I hold you tight, gently wiping each tear from your face. You can trust Me that the brightness of a new day is coming. I will release to you amidst the soreness of your breaking heart, more revelation and truth. From this place of healing you will find the breakthrough for which you have been praying. I will be the

breakthrough for you. I am the God of your breakthrough. So stop striving, dear one. Stay abiding…in the Vine."

Love the Vinedresser

Chapter 24

« The Framework Of Breakthrough For Much Loved Sons And Daughters »

"This resurrection life your received from God (as His much loved son, daughter) is not a timid, grave-tending life. It's adventurously expectant, greeting God with a child-like 'What's next, Papa?' God's Spirit touches our spirits and confirms who we really are. We know Who He is, and we know who we are: Father and children." Romans 8:15-17 MSG (My emphasis in parenthesis)

READ Romans 8

The framework for breakthrough is the beginning for reigning in life.

As I have prayed asking Holy Spirit for wisdom, my heart has been soaking in the truth surrounding one's true identity found in Christ, in the Vine.

Can I share and see if it bears witness with you at this time in your life?

May this be some encouragement to NOT give up.

So to begin, picture three empty frames that anyone could write out their prayers and needs for a change. The actual framework is the solution to breakthrough in three levels. I realize you cannot put God or His ways of working in a box, but bear with me as I try to share what He has been dropping into my spirit.

Each frame is based on what and God says, and who you are becoming, not in who you are not right now.

FOOT SOLDIER

This first frame identifies you as a foot soldier. You are beginning to understand your identity in Him and you are walking in this truth. Like a soldier (Ephesians 6) you have these long spikes in your shoes and know how to stand fast, and how to walk. These spikes dig deep into the soil of the promises of God. You face your problems and needs walking in these promises and trusting the manifestation of provision.

WARRIOR

From foot soldier there is this transformation to warrior. This vessel of the King rises to wield the sword of the Word with power tearing down strongholds in heavenly places, praying at all times. The warrior moves swiftly with power, with the Father's Heart of love. What could take years to change could take minutes just by speaking God's heart to others and walking in the authority His love brings.

MUCH LOVED SON-DAUGHTER

This is such an intimate place knowing you are His son, His daughter in Christ. I see it in my mind as someone who walks with quiet confidence and assurance as they know their inheritance. They understand they are alive with Christ and made to sit with Him in the heavenly places. They truly know they don't have to strive but abide in embracing what the Spirit is actively doing in their life. Romans 8:15-17 in the Message expresses so well what I am trying to express here:

"This resurrection life your received from God (as His much loved son, daughter) is not a timid, grave-tending life. It's adventurously expectant, greeting God with a child-like 'What's next, Papa?' God's Spirit touches our spirits and confirms who we really are. We know Who He is, and we know who we are: Father and children. And we know we are going to get what's coming to us—an unbelievable inheritance!" (My emphasis in parenthesis).

May I encourage you to embrace Him in the process of your breakthrough. Faith supersedes the reality of what you face. The pain you may feel are the birth pains of breakthrough. Holy Spirit is in you helping you along the way.

Declaration: Thank you God that every day I can lay every detail of my needs before you as you transform me and bring the breakthroughs for which I am praying.

Listen To The Vinedresser:

"Come here my precious Child and let this revelation infuse your spirit with hope, life, and renewed purpose. I have not called you as a pauper to live by the traditions of men and rudiments of a fearful world, living in a performance based system. I've loved you forward as royalty. Come sit in My Vineyard and listen to My Heart that beats with empowering love for you."

"Like an earthly father I've called you forth to simply learn how to walk with Me, knowing who you are in this garden. I've called you home, out of the chains of dark shifting shadows into My radiant light. My tender Mercy has extended an open door to enter into My presence and to experience true satisfying love. I've grafted you into the Vine with all the benefits to grow in favor with your dreams and desires."

"Now I'm calling you forth as my foot soldier who truly knows how to walk in your identity to reign. With spikes of truth planted in the soil of My promises, you are meant to walk through the battlefield of process with progress."

"Next, watch Me grant access from foot soldier to transformation into a stalwart Warrior who walks in My love. You come from your rightful place of victory that I secured for you. You are the Warrior who I've commissioned to

tear asunder the highest principalities and authorities in rebellion under the heavenly realms. You walk out The Father's Heart, My love, with authority, flowing in and through you as MY sanctioned mighty champion, praying at all times in the Spirit, wielding the sword of Truth, My Words."

╬

"Now, my dear foot soldier, warrior, hero of families, regions, and nations, come farther into this Vineyard to see the full inheritance I give you as you abide, dwell and rest. Now My lover, My friend, sit in this saving grace seat, in the Vine at my right Hand. Listen as I soak you in deeper truth, tender words of passionate love that I have for you. This is who you are and who you are becoming. You are Mine, child, clothed with My Strength to walk through the process of any mess while you clearly trust I'm for you and not against you."

"Do you hear what I am saying? I am so proud of you. You are wonderfull, you are radiant. You are… My much loved Son. You are My much loved Daughter. So abide. Don't strive here in the Vine."

Love the Vinedresser

Chapter 25

« The Place Of Breakthrough »

"Don't allow the foxes of religion, and weeds of fear mess up the garden of your love for me." The Vinedresser

READ 2 Samuel 5:17-25

You can push back the fear and frustration and find the place of breakthrough.

Your days have purpose amidst weary days. Yes! From despair to devastation, you can still find purpose! The process can be the pressure to produce fruit in your life that someone else needs.

It's part of a shift. It's time for the Father's Heart to be released to you! Someone in the dark is waiting for you to speak this word to them.

The key to go through this process is found in this simple thought:

Don't forget what God has spoken to you as you journey through the process of life. Hold on to what He said. What He shared in the light will be needed for someone who is in the dark. Personal breakthrough releases corporate breakthrough. Yes, you are the breakthrough

God has this wonderful way of using the pressures of everyday life to bring PROGRESS. He sees you seated with Him, in Christ, as His much loved Son, His much loved daughter. You are His gem. He sees you as a diamond. Maybe you feel like you are in the rough, but He is ready to release you to shine.

God is all about progress, not about constriction nor restraint.

So I encourage you. Remember what God has spoken to you. Hold on to the promises of God. They are 'yes' and 'amen' in Christ. And you are in Christ as you have confessed and believed in Him.

So can I share this with you as a way to say...I understand...I'm sorry it can be so painful. But take heart.

Amidst the squeeze and pressure you feel, He is there. His Word says He perfects that which concerns Him (Psalm 138). You concern Him. After all He is the author and perfecter of your faith! (Hebrews 12:2).

The Word says His promises have abundant life attached. He is all about you walking in joy and peace.

So go to the real place of breakthrough, the Word and hold on to His promises, the very words He has spoken to you. His promises are 'yes' and 'Amen'... Stay faithful and strapped to the Vine.

I believe God is raising up people like you to go from weary days to wonder-filled days, from gory stories to glory stories.

You are part of the answer for the Kingdom of heaven to be released on the earth.

Stay in the soil of His promises amidst the process so that you can be that ripe fruit, spilling forth the 'sweet wine (juice)', to bring refreshment and healing everywhere you go.

Declaration: My Father is all about my dreams and bringing me to the place of breakthrough...inside me!

Listen To The Vinedresser:

"Come here child to the place of breakthrough inside My garden. Consume My love. Let's dance together in worship. This is where My lover's

dream and get filled with sweet revelation wine. To move in this motion, you have to release the burdens that are slowing you down. Come My lover and be embraced now by the rhythm of My grace."

✠

"No matter your age, I will release you into your Kingdom assignment with My mark of excellence. Watch for Me to drop more extraordinary wisdom to explode the creativity that I put in your DNA. Witty ideas and extraordinary solutions to pains of the world will bring resources. You will have the finances to continue bringing heaven's ideas to earth as you display the favor of the Kingdom in the marketplace."

"Stand always in integrity displaying My intentionality for truth. Take care of yourself child. Rest often in the field of My love and tender affection. Trust Me. I am the One behind the fulfillment of your dream for the Kingdom."

"Watch for the fruit. Watch what I do to bloom in you more of My Presence. Do you see what is happening? Inside you is the Vineyard displaying My Kingdom with the smell of harvest! As you consistently tend to the garden of My love in your heart, everywhere you go you bring the sweet smelling fragrance of My Kingdom. Every place I lead you, others will breathe in the exquisite aroma."

"So understand My dear beloved, as I grafted you into the Vine, Christ in you is the Vineyard. Contend and maintain your heart relationship with Me. Don't allow the foxes of religion, and weeds of fear mess up the garden of your love for me. Watch what I do in your life. You will be My hands and My voice to speak healing as creative miracles will be the norm. Others will feed off the fruit of your Vineyard and be released to their true identity in Me. Walk where I lead with no striving. Simply be found abiding in The Vine, in the garden, in the place of breakthrough."

Love the Vinedresser

Chapter 26

« It's Your Turn For Breakthrough »

"So, what does all this mean? If God has determined to stand with us, tell me, who then could ever stand against us?" Romans 8:31 TPT

READ John 14

I see so many crying out for God to move in restoration, healing, finances, family issues.

So many are clinging to the word shift or breakthrough.

A thought occurred to me the other day.

You don't have to wait for the shift or the breakthrough. That is who you are! It is the result of the finished work of Jesus Christ.

As I was putting a finish to a Video Series, The Place of Breakthrough, I was reminded of simple truths from the Word which makes sense to all of these breakthrough thoughts. It comes down to this verse:

"So, what does all this mean? If God has determined to stand with us, tell me, who then could ever stand against us? For God has proved his love by giving us his greatest treasure, the gift of his Son. And since God freely offered him up as the sacrifice for us all, he certainly won't withhold from us anything else he has to give." Romans 8:31-32 TPT

You are made to be more than a conqueror. It is your turn to rise up and (move forward trusting God) amidst the process knowing He has progress for you as you cling to the Vine.

Whether life for you is messy or miserable, I have one thing to say to you.

It's your turn.

Yes, I said it's your turn for breakthrough, shifts, and healing.

It's a prophetic word in the air from the Heart of God, your Father. Whether you hear 'shift' or 'bridge', it's time for God's sons and daughters to arise and get ready for His move. He is working in the lives of those who have faithfully stayed 'in the vine', in intimate contact with God.

I do understand how it can feel like you are hitting your head against the same wall that separates you from your hopes and dreams. I'm sorry the pain can be so intense at times that you feel there is no hope or you are just flat tired.

I also know that God is so for you. You are the shift in the atmosphere! It is your time.

I wanted to share something that the Holy Spirit dropped into my heart after seeing a shift in healing with my son-in-law in a hospital room. It's something that God is doing in many hearts like yours to see the results you desire in your marriage, your children, and yes, even in your finances.

The Holy Spirit said being a changer of atmospheres comes first in your own home. Yes, right around the people with whom you live and experience life—friction and all.

Declaration: Jesus, by Your death and resurrection on the Cross, I know it's my turn to walk in healing and restoration as I reign today as Your much loved Son, Your Much Loved daughter, son.

Listen to the Vinedresser:

"It's your turn now child. Don't you know that being hidden with Me in the Vine puts you on My side. If you are on my side, who can be against you? How could you lose? I have embraced your condition and provided a solution in the gift of My Son on the Cross and now alive in you. His blood makes the way for an open door everyday into the Vineyard of my Love."

"It's your turn now to rise up as my much loved son, my much loved daughter to walk in triumph as more than conquerors amidst life's troubles. Who would dare tangle with Me or try to snatch you from entering this quiet place of My love, in the Vineyard? I am sticking up for you like one who sticks up for a kid being unfairly picked on by the neighborhood bully."

"No one can snatch you away from My Presence. No one can get in the way of My purpose for you. You're not a sitting duck waiting to be shot out of the water. You are Mine…resting in the protection of My Vine."

"It's your turn now child. Remember this is not about performance or striving. It's about abiding in the place of breakthrough I provided. The majesty of My lavish love demonstrates that you can walk in victory over everything simply by what I accomplished, once and for all, through My Son's death and resurrection."

"It's your turn now. You are no longer hidden gems. I have orchestrated the stage for you to come out and shine. You may not be on the nightly newscast, but you're spreading my powerful love with signs and wonders will be broadcasted for MY GLORY. You will not be seeking a stage but simply a Word from My Spirit. You will walk in MY Power to tear down strongholds

in heavenly places as you reflect the goodness and mercy of Me to those you meet every day."

"It's your turn. I have opened doors to you to walk in territory that once was dominated by the enemy. Just your entering through these doors will change the atmosphere for my Glory to flow. You will walk in the confidence knowing that any attack from the enemy cannot shake you off the Vine of My Son's love for you. You will no longer feel stuck between two sides of an issue. You will operate with confidence knowing that absolutely nothing can get between you and God's loving purpose for your life."

╬

"It is your turn. My Glory is being reflected by one spark of revival in a heart to another. These are not gloom and doom days, my child. Look for the glory stories and radical testimonies…Eyes that see. Ears that hear. Bodies healed. Minds restored. Orphans becoming sons and daughters. Salvation coming to thousands in your sphere of influence."

"It's your turn my beloved."

Love The Vinedresser

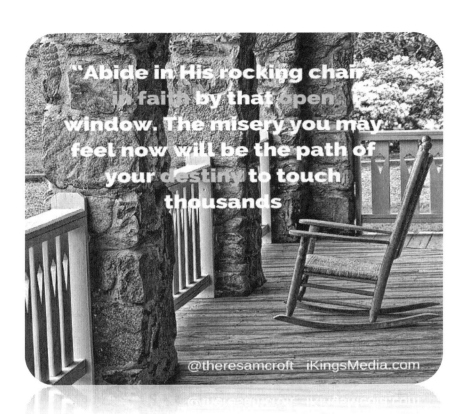

"Abide in His rocking chair in faith by that open window. The misery you may feel now will be the path of your destiny to touch thousands

Chapter 27

« Fresh Start In The Vine »

"Whether life for you is messy or miserable, I have one thing to say to you. It's your turn..."

READ Ephesians 2

I pray as you get to this chapter in this devotional that something will start to resonate in your heart. These kind of words from God talking to you might really be something new. I believe as you shift toward belief in your mind, that the word of the Holy Spirit starts to reveal to you more of Him. It's a design, a frequency, a dazzling move of heaven in your heart.

Now, let's be real. This is not a word based on some 'fuzzy' feeling or dancing through the St. Arbucks (Starbucks) coffee high emotions. No. God's voice is so real. The Holy Spirit can speak to you so clearly amidst the chaotic emotions of your heart.

Let me try to explain more.

Last year we received a call, that every parent fears. Our son-in-law was pinned in his truck one early morning. The resounding prayers that went up from our Kingdom Messenger Network of Social Media Prayer was tremendous. He is recovering now and is a walking miracle

Ok…so amidst all THIS (and other issues) what does the Holy Spirit say? Basically it's this:

'The shift' is on for you to walk from a warrior to a son, a daughter of the King. I truly believe God is pulling people from the wreckage of fear and devastation of tragedy and raising them up as beacons of light. From upheavals in marriages, to crashes of finances, nothing is too difficult for God. Messes do not move Him off His throne and make Him powerless. Out of anguish often comes breakthrough when you cling to Him.

Yes…now. God broke it down like this:

Forget the week to week 'pay check' of stress. Make this your declaration! Better yet, get a pen and write this one down:

Declaration: "As a son or daughter of THE KING I will walk from the place of victory, from heaven, encountering Him each day. I expect my going forth to contain days of blessings, week to week wealth, (not just finances, but health, peace, wisdom…shalom), month to month glory stories, year to year experiences of His unrelenting love. I am expecting great chapters of faith in this coming year. It's who I am in Christ, in the Vine!"

Listen To The Vinedresser:

"My beloved. You can open the chapters of who you are, who you have been, and who you want to be, in your life to Me. Allow Me to rewrite the text. Written in red are My mysteries for you to uncover. Like panning for gold, I leave great nuggets for those who search Me out."

"Not all see. But I have chosen to open your eyes. So search for Me this year, child, like you have never searched before. Look with the eyes of your heart. Lay the pieces of your shattered life with all the hurt, shame, and betrayal before Me. I am the One to give you a fresh start. I will put you back together."

"So go ahead, open the book of your heart. I have the pen. I write 'brilliant', 'wonderful', 'healthy', 'good', 'Revivalist', 'My precious One', 'Hero of families', 'the Breaker-anointed one', the 'leader of peace,' the 'compassionate

child', the 'one who loves well', 'My son, My daughter', in the chapters of your life, to name just a few."

"I am here to give you a fresh start. Be alert to the Presence of My Spirit gently moving in you. From the place of the chaotic emotions of the process, I gently speak peace and hope. I will help you uncover resplendent mysterious from My heart to you! So now, knowing you are a true son, daughter, of Mine, walk carrying My radiant love to others to help them find their identity in Me, in the Vine."

✠

"I love you so much. You are so wonderful. You are leaving the footprints of My Kingdom everywhere you go. Thank you."

"Now rest. Dwell. Stay. Don't strive. Abide in the Vine!"

Love the Vinedresser

Chapter 28

« The Breaker Anointing »

"And to the angel of the church in Philadelphia write, 'These things say He who is holy, He who is true, He who has the key of David, He who opens and not one shuts and no one opens." Revelation 3:7 NKJ

READ Matthew 16:13-20

I believe the breaker-anointing is in you. And God gives you...keys.

I cannot shake these words of keys.

Recently, I had something happen that was like an open vision. I'll spare you the details but it goes along with something that has been on my heart about hope, influence, and changing your belief-thinking. Thoughts like this:

The ones with the most influence have the most hope. You get hope unlimited in the womb of intimacy with Jesus.

Hope can be thrown out to others like a seed of influence. This kind of hope shows others that they can have the same hope as they abide, rest, dwell, in the Vine.

So, in essence this is one set of keys that God lets you enter heaven in the spirit and release on earth. This is what being a breaker-anointed messenger means. I believe He has some real keys to give you too, such as to offices, vehicles, homes etc. I have received testimonies of this in the past year and am expecting more.

I also believe He has keys to the supernatural realm for you now to mirror what's in heaven. You take that reflection and shine it on your circumstances. And then watch! You become a magnet for all of God's goodness, grace, and mercy for more! Reach and grab this by faith and belief as you pray, "Open the eyes of my heart, Lord!"

Someone needs a real glimpse of heaven. Someone needs the healing and hope of heaven. You have the keys. This demonstration happens first around those closest to whom you live. If you can display all of God's goodness and fruit of His Spirit right in your home, it becomes all the more easier when you walk out the door. From Wal-Mart to Home Depot, you are a shining light of His love that splashes on everyone around you. This could be as simple as a kind word or a helping hand. The world is looking for this kind of messenger who calls themselves Christian.

Declaration: I can be the hope of heaven. He is giving me the keys to shine His Glory on everyone I come in contact.

Listen to the Vinedresser:

"You forgot something dear child. The key to intimacy is with Me. In this secret place you can hear what I am saying to you about your problems, your circumstances, your trials. So I beckon you again to come soak in the Holy Spirit healing balm found in My Vineyard of My tender care."

"Here is one key. Here is one promise. 'I will never leave you nor forsake you.' You are not invisible to Me even though you feel you are to those around you."

"I remain with a heart fully toward you with the intentionality of the goodness of My overflowing love. Take that one key child and speak it out loud. Your breakthrough is one word of My promise spoken out loud by faith and belief. This one key opens the eyes of your heart so you can see and hear the resounding YES of heaven."

"Now, beloved, you are ready to engage in the spirit realm where you will have free and complete access to My Kingdom as I send you out as My breaker-anointing messenger. You will be the door of hope. That hope carries the influences which shifts atmospheres. You will be the one I entrust to handle the wealth of the storehouses in heaven as a faithful steward releasing resources wisely."

╬

"You will produce My radical passion for jewels of heaven with souls saved, healing, miracles, training, equipping, and producing disciples who carry extra ordinary provision. You will use the keys that I give you to enter doors of those who run cities, states, and nations. The Father-heart I give you will be foreign to many you meet behind these closed doors. What would take years to accomplish will take minutes as you embrace them with the majesty of My love."

"More doors will open. More walls will come down. Watch this happen in those closest to you first. Get ready, My beloved. You are My hidden gem who I am ready to shine through. You've been through the fire. You've stood the test by resting in My love. You are the one I choose with all the keys to open more doors so My Kingdom will be released with no more barriers between heaven and earth, earth and heaven. It all starts here with no striving, but simply abiding, in the Vine."

Love the Vinedresser

Chapter 29

« Give Thanks »

"But I will give all my thanks to you, Lord, for you to make everything right in the end." Psalm 7:17 TPT

READ Psalm 100

What is one weapon that helps you tap into the heart of God while at the same time defeats debilitating circumstances in your life?

Thanksgiving.

It almost seems so simple yet so difficult to do at times.

But as I study and allow the Holy Spirit to direct me, the truth of thanksgiving comes to light.

For one, thanksgiving carries an attitude of honor and humility.

God gives you a gift of relationship with Him. When you thank Him, you are set on a journey to know God in a more intimate relationship. You discover His kind intentions for you. You come to understand The Father's Heart where He desires to give you every good and perfect gift.

I hear you thinking. "But what about all this 'crap' I'm facing?" (If that word offends sorry. This is what I hear).

God did not cause the difficult circumstances that have crashed on you. He can help you walk in victory through it. This is where thanksgiving is a weapon to disarm the enemy and you tap into the heart of God.

"We don't engage battle by focusing on the devil. We keep our focus on the King and His Kingdom, and the devil cannot help but be unseated by God's ever-increasing government released through our lives."

Bill Johnson

God is intentional for progress through the pressures of the process in your life. Because of that you can be sure He will come through for you. Better yet, He can bring justice to your situation as you continue to focus on Him.

"But I will give all my thanks to you, Lord, for you make everything right in the end. I will sing my highest praise to the God of the Highest Place!" Psalm 7:17 TPT

I am being reminded in my own current situation to thank Him. I see how as I offer thanksgiving even amidst an adverse situation, this can be my sacrifice to Him. It's like I lay my heart on the altar saying, "I trust you, Lord. So I will offer up a sacrifice of praise and thanksgiving."

This sets the stage for the atmosphere around me to change. I go from focusing on my problem to looking to God to handle the issue. This helps me stay aware of His Presence and His promises for my life. It also can supernaturally change my problem.

Thanksgiving sanctifies, brings His judgement, and keeps you in the center of what God is doing. Thanksgiving helps you to focus on Him so that you shift your awareness from the reality of your circumstances to heaven's reality.

Here's the key. Thanksgiving gives you, His much loved son, His much loved daughter, audience with the King! Thanksgiving releases the strength of Heaven into your circumstances.

So will you use this gift to thank Him?

Declaration: Thank you for allowing me know You in relationship. I thank God for His love and commitment to me in every situation (name your specific situation) I face. You are bringing me through and arming me with a testimony of Your faithfulness in my life.

Listen To The Vinedresser:

╬

"Dear child, I hear you crying for breakthrough. You are tired of your circumstances and pressures that are taking you out for the count. I hear you plead for help. Your complaints have hit my ears. Listen. I have a weapon I am going to give you that you can carry at all times. Think it not strange that this sounds so easy, yet seems so difficult for you to walk out."

"The weapon lies in what you speak. Can you offer up a sacrifice of praise even if your life seems to be in a downward spiral. Contend my dear one. I have put My Spirit in you to win this battle. I draw near to you as you draw near to Me. From this intimate relationship you have this tool to destroy the attacks on your back. When you give Me thanks you usher in an atmosphere where the small becomes great. You tap into my heart and disarm the enemy."

"Give thanks. Offer up praise. Even if it is a sacrifice. Imagine how pleased I am to see you put your humble heart on the altar. How sweet that aroma is to Me. This is the beginning of your breakthrough. Don't try to figure all this out with your mind. I love to slap righteousness on what the world calls ridiculous!"

"I love you Child. I am always moving amidst the process for your benefit. Now take your hands off the thing that wants to strangle your hope and believe in Me and My promises. I give you every good and perfect gift. I desire to see you prosper and succeed. Enter in now. No striving. Abide in the Vine."

Love the Vinedresser

Chapter 30

« Breakthrough Thoughts In The Vine »

"He is our example and father, for in God's presence he believed that God can raise the dead and call into being things that don't even exist yet." Romans 4:17 TPT

READ Romans 4

His greatest breakthrough for you is closer than you think. You may be inches away and shrink away?

Sometimes the enemy kicks his heels to stir up some dust so we won't see what's in front of us. Dig deep. Hold on. Someone else's greatest breakthrough is on the other end, not to mention your own!

Or, when you find what you thought was most dear to you is lost, you often find what is most dear to you. Jesus!

This is the key. You can rely on the Holy Spirit, not your emotions, to step away from fear into faith (trust and belief).

These are some breakthrough thoughts for you on a day where I was sitting listening to some great worship while my husband sat next to me praying and resting.

Do you know how much the Father takes great pleasure in you, while you cling to Him amidst the battles and squeamish messes in you walk as His Messenger? I encourage you to look with eyes of your heart, your spirit, as you see what seems like dead ends on your journey of faith. The let downs are often the weights that are used by God to build your muscles in faith, hope, and yes, love. He builds the foundation so you can handle the destiny He has for you!

Never stop believing God's promises over your life. Continue to speak declarations of what He says about you. Be thankful amidst the process.

╬

What seems as impossible could simply be resistance from the enemy.

Declaration: I will listen to God, who can call those things that are not, as though they are. I will walk in faith in Him no matter how far the breakthrough seems. His promises are yes and amen!

Listen to the Vinedresser:

"Beloved, never stop believing My promises over your life. Even if it looks like all odds are against you, tenaciously hang on to My 'yes' which I proclaim over you. I can call into being things that don't even exist yet. Look with eyes of faith, My child. When you see a problem, look with your spirit eyes. Do you see My Hand? I am paving new ground for my promises to bloom and producing fruit of provision. In the midst of the pressure of the process you are becoming a warrior, a carrier of My presence."

"The fruit of your obedience is beginning to bloom."

"In the midst of the battles, come away often and sit in My Vineyard. Gaze into My loving eyes. Be embraced by My Presence. I will not waver in My devotion and care for you. In this deep quiet place, I can stir your faith and remind you how I see you. I can teach you how to walk by My Spirit and be familiar with my Voice."

"Your faith in My Son imparts My righteousness to you. With this comes the knowing in your heart that I see you flawless, all because of the finished work of The Anointed One, Jesus. So rest, my child, and enjoy true and lasting

peace in my garden. I am thrilled to lavish My marvelous kindness on you in this abiding place."

"As you experience My Glory, get ready for incredible joy to burst forth in your innermost being. As I celebrate you, beloved, and not merely tolerate you, you can keep on walking in hope as you experience more territory of my love. Do you see it? Look with the eyes of your heart. No need to strive for all of this My beloved. Simply Abide… in the Vine."

Love the Vinedresser

Chapter 31

« Living In The Sweet Spot »

"In this sweet spot you reign with abundance of joy and protection. You live in habitation being well taken care of by My supply of unending, unfailing love."

READ John 4

Does living in the sweet spot mean you are living on the beach, or in some remote cabin in the woods?

Maybe that is simply where you would like to be now.

I understand you are tired with the constant barrage of bills needing to be paid, relationships hitting the rocks, or your body crashing with pain. I am sorry that you are falling on some treacherous times with chaotic emotions.

I do believe amidst the battle you can find a 'sweet spot' of living your life by design, not default, in the Vine.

This study of being in the Vine, in the sweet spot, started almost five years ago in the mountains as God was speaking to me about being in the Vine and living in the sweet spot of divine destiny. It was here that I began listening to the Vinedresser of my life and writing out these *"Listen To The Vinedresser"* words.

From John 15 with the Vinedresser taking care of the garden of my heart, I learned set-backs are really set-ups by God for upgrade. All of heaven is cheering you on and watching to see what you will do with what He has given you. You bring heaven to earth. Your prayers break chains off yourself and others. Your love from Him shows others more about the Father Heart of God!

Finally, living in the sweet spot means you are a carrier of Kingdom advancement. You manage the interior of your life, your own vineyard, in your heart. Replace pressure in the process with prayer. Walk in freedom of who you are in Him, not fear. As you manage your heart, the Holy Spirit can rest in greater measure for you to be a messenger of Kingdom breakthrough in your sphere of influence.

Being in the sweet spot in not about a place, really, but about a position of your heart. As you learn your identity in Him as a much loved daughter, a much loved son, you realize that you can be in the sweet spot no matter WHAT is going on around you.

Would you like to experience that now instead of waiting? Do you believe that Jesus said He promised you abundant life…right now? This is not a performance act. This is not jumping through hoops A through D. This is about understanding that being in the sweet spot is really about who you are…in the Vine!

I believe God is raising up people like you to truly be in the sweet spot.

Declaration: I am in my season for the sweet spot. It is the position of my hear in You with Your Hand on my life. I will let go and trust You to help me live always in the Vine, always in the sweet spot.

Listen To The Vinedresser:

"My child, I hear your cries above the noise of your rattling emotions and treacherous circumstances. No matter where you are in your life, you can always find a home in My Heart, in this garden. In here you can be found in My glory, no matter how feeble and overwhelmed you may feel."

"For in My Vineyard is the only true sweet spot in life. I am your shelter, your safe place. You can always hide your heart in My splendor shadow, full of

Holy Spirit dew. You are My beloved. I take good care of lovers of My Presence."

"In this sweet spot you reign with abundance of joy and protection. You live in habitation being taken care of by My supply of unending, unfailing love. Your praise from this spot attracts all my grace and favor. Being in the sweet spot is more of a position of being constantly aware of the Vineyard I planted in your heart."

✠

"Your life in this sweet spot is My poem written to fulfill My purpose in you. As I make your heart sing like a harp, your life becomes a beautiful song to Me. I carefully write each stanza displaying My majestic love. As you listen to My tune, the Holy Spirit and follow His beat, you fulfill your destiny in the Vine, the sweet spot."

"So you have the opportunity to share this paradise love gift that I placed in your heart every day with others. Forgive. Trust Me. Daily in the sweet spot, in My Presence, you can put away the foxes of fear, and the ox of offense, that want to destroy your garden. You can live above the fray of evil around you knowing your heart is secure in My wrap-around presence.

"So dear child. My Vineyard is in you! Abide. No performance, no strive. It really is who you are…in the Vine."

Love the Vinedresser

Conclusion

One final thought as you come to the end of this devotional. I have discovered two things while writing these Holy Spirit words. The first is simple.

Many times I have gone back over these *"Listen To The Vinedresser"* words and come away refreshed. The Holy Spirit has an amazing way of lifting your head and giving you hope. So, I pray you will not put this devotional away after you read it.

The second thing I've discovered is how powerful these words are if spoken out loud over someone. My husband and I have had the chance to minister to many Kingdom Messengers through the years. The Holy Spirit has often directed me to find a Vinedresser word as my husband would speak life over them. Whether in person or on the phone, I can't explain the electricity we have felt in the air as I would read a Vinedresser word over a tender heart. No doubt, this is one way to share a declaration over a family member or friend by reading a Vinedresser Word out loud to them.

Thank you for entering into the Vineyard to spend time with the Vinedresser in this devotional. I pray you will take care of the vineyard in your own heart by contending for His Presence, no matter what you may be facing. Every day you can bring the Vineyard of God's love to those you around you and they can be refreshed by the fruit in your devotion to Jesus.

May you always remember to walk as His much loved Son, His much loved daughter. Remember to abide, no striving, as you pursue more of the Vinedresser!

About The Author

Theresa Croft, 'the media messenger', is a wife, mom and a Kingdom revivalist. She is creator of the #inthevine and "*Listen To The Vinedresser*" Movement online. She excels as in Social Media Marketing and as an online Influencer. She is also an author, and Life Speaker. You can view the heart behind this media messenger by going to her Facebook page, facebook.com/TheresaMCroft, or being a part of her ezine family with weekly messages of hope and Kingdom life. She is dedicated to spread the "no strive, abide in the Vine" message through media and speaking events.

Follow the Theresa On The Web:

iKingsMedia.com

facebook.com/TheresaMCroft

youtube.com/c/TheresaCroft

instagram.com/theresacroft/

twitter.com/TheresaMCroft

Made in the USA
Lexington, KY
29 December 2016